AMAZING AYODHYA

Dear Susan,
Mataj & Abhra

Hope you enjoy reading this
book as much as I enjoyed
writing it -

lots of love

जय श्री राम
जय हनुमान

26 July '22
Florida

AMAZING AYODHYA

*The Splendid Ancient City of
Lord Rama*

Neena Rai

BLOOMSBURY
NEW DELHI • LONDON • OXFORD • NEW YORK • SYDNEY

BLOOMSBURY INDIA
Bloomsbury Publishing India Pvt. Ltd
Second Floor, LSC Building No. 4, DDA Complex, Pocket C – 6 & 7,
Vasant Kunj, New Delhi 110070

BLOOMSBURY, BLOOMSBURY INDIA and the Diana logo
are trademarks of Bloomsbury Publishing Plc

First published in India 2021
This edition published 2021

ISBN: PB: 978-93-90358-87-8; e-Book: 978-93-90358-03-8
2 4 6 8 10 9 7 5 3 1

Typeset in Manipal Technologies Limited
Printed and bound in India

To find out more about our authors and books, visit www.bloomsbury.com and sign
up for our newsletters

My maternal grandmother and I

To my naani (maternal grandmother), Maitreyi Rai, granddaughter of the famous zamindar, Hari Narayan Singh. Named after the legendary female Hindu philosopher and composer of the Vedas, Maitreyi, true to her name, not only quenches my thirst for spiritual and scriptural knowledge but also fuels it by continuously discussing various interesting facets of dharmic treatises.

May the glory of Shri Rama and his consort,
Devi Sita, forever be recited.
May all devotees rejoice in the freeing
of the birthplace of *Rama Lalla*.
May Ayodhya return to its former splendour.

CONTENTS

Preface xiii
Transliteration Guide xv
Why Did I Write This Book? xxii
Manglacharan xxv

Introduction 1

PART I: ANTIQUITY:
ANSWERING THE WHO AND WHEN

1 Who Established Ayodhya? 5

2 Who Is Manu? 6

3 When Was Ayodhya Established? 15

4 Unbroken Link of the Solar Dynasty
from Satya Yuga to Treta Yuga 16

PART II: 'LOCATION. LOCATION. LOCATION':
ANSWERING THE WHERE AND WHAT?

5 What Was Ayodhya? 23

6 Where Was Ayodhya Located? 32

7 Where Was Kosala? 34

8 How Big Was Kosala? 38

9   Was Kosala a Kingdom or an Empire?   40

10   How Many Kings Were under Dasharatha's
     Dominion?   43

        PART III: SHAPES, PLANS AND LAYOUTS:
          THE EXTERIOR DESIGN OF AYODHYA

11   What Was the Shape of Ayodhya?   57

12   What Was the Size of Ayodhya?   60

13   How Populated Was Ayodhya?   67

14   How Was Ayodhya Designed to
     Protect It from Enemies?   69

          PART IV: DESIGNER DETAILS:
        DESCRIBING THE INSIDES OF AYODHYA

15   The Roadways of Ayodhya   92

16   The Buildings of Ayodhya   101

17   The Shape and Structure of Residences   110

18   The Palaces of Ayodhya   135

          PART V: WEAPONS IN AYODHYA:
            THE MYSTERIOUS *SHATAGHNII*

19   What Kind of Weaponry Was Visible in
     Ayodhya?   177

20   Decoding the aTTaala   179

21   Decoding the Mysterious *shataghnii*   190

PART VI: ANIMALS IN AYODHYA

22 Chaturangi Sena   216

23 The akshouhiNii   218

24 Useful Animals Abounding Ayodhya   229

25 Importing Horses and Hippopotamuses   232

26 Importing and Breeding of Elephants   242

27 The Birds of Ayodhya   248

28 Other Pets at Prince Rama's Palace   261

29 Why Does Devi Sita Request Lord Rama
    to Get Her the Golden Deer?   265

    Phalashruti   269
    Afterword   272
    Sources   284
    Bibliography   287
    About the Author   289

PREFACE

In order to understand the avatars we worship, it is often important to understand how the life and times were in their yuga. For that purpose, *Amazing Ayodhya* is an attempt in gaining knowledge of Ayodhya. It is a book aimed at shedding light on its design, its architecture and other details in order to understand the life and times of the Ramayanic Era. It is an attempt to describe the splendour of Ayodhya in as many details as possible.

Amazing Ayodhya has been compiled after many years of my research on Hindu scriptures. The researched scriptures were not only limited to the Ramayana but also extended to other ancient Hindu works like *Shilpa Shastra* (treatise on art, craft and sculpture), *Vastu Shastra* (treatise on town planning and house making), Ayurveda (science of extending life), Bhagavad Gita (the song of God) and Puranas, etc. In order to read and research the Ramayana and to describe its amazing details, I started learning Sanskrit in 2016. Fast forward to 2020, I am still learning Sanskrit and reading the scriptures.

To appropriately present the content of this researched book, I have supplemented the matter with images of *shlokas* from the Valmiki Ramayana along with their translations.

Apart from images and translations, further descriptions are given so that the reader is able to comprehend what is being discussed. In many parts of this book, I have discussed the meaning of words in Sanskrit and how certain explanations of *shlokas* have been arrived at. This is specifically done for *shlokas* containing certain words whose meanings may vary due to their translation. This particular manner of crafting a book is done on purpose, so that a person reading this book will not only have access to the minute details of ancient Ayodhya in English but also the Sanskrit verses and words that describe those details. This process will enable the reader to not only understand the content and verify its source but also increase their knowledge of Sanskrit vocabulary.

The language used in writing this book is kept simple and basic so that curious-minded children can easily read this book. The book also contains various images to illustrate the meaning of the terms that are being discussed so that a young reader is able to grasp the content fully.

As far as possible, I have given credit to all the images used in the book. Images are mostly from copyright-free sources with the exception of a few. The books and articles I have referred to are listed in the Bibliography section at the end of this book.

TRANSLITERATION GUIDE

Progress on the spiritual path and acquiring deep yogic knowledge came easy to me when I lived in India. Thanks to the influence and *sanskaar* of my family, growing up, I was surrounded by learned pundits, yoga teachers and gurus from whom I imbibed knowledge and guidance. *Sanskaar* loosely translates to good virtues, values and ethical conduct.

I was 18 when I first moved abroad and after that I lived on and off in India and various other countries. In the years I lived abroad as non-resident Indian (NRI), I felt dharmic guidance disappear, and gradually I slipped into a vacuum of spiritual knowledge. To fill that vacuum, I resorted to gaining knowledge from books. Since I was more comfortable in English, I studied various esoteric yogic books in the same language. One summer, while visiting India, I had a conversation with my *naani* (maternal grandmother) about a certain evolved yogic practice called 'Nada Yoga'. Every time I mentioned the word Nada, she would politely enunciate 'naa-da'. Even after hearing my grandmother a few times, I kept repeating the mistake as I was more excited about sharing my experience. After a while, my mother who was a witness to this discussion, noticed that I was not registering what was being told so she intervened and said, '*Naani* is telling you that your pronunciation is wrong. You are pronouncing the word "naa-da" as "Naa-Daa". That is wrong.'

I felt a bit cheated on hearing my mother's words. Cheated, because I pronounced it the way I was supposed to pronounce in English. Since my *naani* knew much more than I, there was no doubt in my mind that my pronunciation was wrong. Considering that I was only exposed to these Sanskrit terms in English and not in Sanskrit or Hindi, my pronunciation suffered. At that point, I felt miffed with the book. I felt that while it gave me correct knowledge, why did it deprive me of correct pronunciation?

This incident made me realise that I needed to relearn Sanskrit and that is exactly what I did once I moved back to India. So that no young, curious mind feels deprived of the correct pronunciations, for this book I have given, to the best of my knowledge, the Sanskrit *shlokas* and their transliterations in ITRANS format. While I am no expert at transliteration, I felt that I would be doing injustice to the readers if I did not transliterate. A transliteration map and an index of transliterated words, which are commonly used in this book, are also given.

What Is Transliteration?

Sanskrit puts a lot of emphasis on correct pronunciation of words as each letter in Sanskrit vibrates at a particular frequency. Specialised combination of words or mantras have the capacity to bring about drastic changes in one's life, if chanted correctly.

A translation provides the meaning of the Sanskrit *shloka*, whereas a transliteration helps you to enunciate the words just as it is enunciated in Sanskrit.

Apart from my personal experience mentioned above, I have transliterated Sanskrit *shlokas* and words to also help readers who are not familiar with the Devanagari script. This would not only help readers understand the script but also be able to pronounce the words correctly through English. In this manner, they would be able to harness the power of the Sanskrit language.

While there are various transliteration systems or schemes in place, the tool I have chosen to go with is the ITRANS system, which I felt was much easier for me to understand. ITRANS stands for Indian languages TRANSliteration. Avinash Chopde is the main person behind this transliteration system.

Transliteration Map

Digits
संख्या

०	0
१	1
२	2
३	3
४	4
५	5
६	6
७	7
८	8
९	9

Vowels
स्वर

अ	a
आ	aa or A
इ	i
ई	ii or I
उ	u
ऊ	uu or U
ऋ	R^i
ॠ	R^I
ऌ	L^i
ॡ	L^I

ए	e
ऐ	ai
ओ	o
औ	au
अं	aM
अः	aH

Consonants
व्यञ्जन

क वर्ग
ka varga

क	ka
ख	kha
ग	ga
घ	gha
ङ	N^a

च वर्ग
cha varga

च	cha
छ	chha
ज	ja
झ	jha
ञ	JNa

ट वर्ग
Ta varga

ट	Ta
ठ	Tha
ड	Da
ढ	Dha
ण	Na

त वर्ग
ta varga

त	ta
थ	tha
द	da
ध	dha
न	na

प वर्ग
pa varga

प	pa
फ	pha
ब	ba
भ	bha
म	ma

अन्तःस्थ
antaHstha

य	ya
र	ra
ल	la
व	va

ऊष्म
UShma

श	sha
ष	shha
स	sa
ह	ha

Conjuncts
संयुक्त वर्ण

क्ष	xa or ksha
ज्ञ	GYa
श्र	shra
त्र	tra
द्य	dya

Specials

ॐ	AUM or OM
ळ	lda or La

Miscellaneous
प्रकीर्ण

क़	qa
ख़	Ka
ग़	Ga
ज़	za
फ़	fa
ड़	.Da
ढ़	.Dha

ग	ga.r
गं	ga.n
आँ	aa.c
डँ	Da.N
ड्	D.h
दुः	duH
ऽ	.a

Here are some sample consonants with vowels as examples.

क का कि की कु कू	ka kaa ki kii ku kuu
स सा सि सी सु सू	sa saa si sii su suu
खृ खे खै खं खः खॉ खँ	khR^I khe khai khaM khaH kha.c kha.N
डे डै डं डः डॉ डँ	De Dai DaM DaH Da.c Da.N

The following is a guide detailing certain Sanskrit words with their transliterations and their commonly used

English spellings in India. The first column has the word in Sanskrit. The second column has the transliterated version and the third column has the word's common Indianised English spelling. They are in random order.

संस्कृत	ITRANS	Indian English
रामः	raamaH or rAmaH	Rama
सीता	sItaa or sItA	Sita
कृष्णः	kR^iShNaH	Krishna
दशरथः	dasharathaH	Dasharatha
कैकेयी	kaikeyI	Kaikeyi
कौशल्या	kaushalyA	Kaushalya
रावणः	rAvaNaH or raavaNaH	Ravana
शत्रुघ्नः	shatrughnaH	Shatrughna
परशुरामः	parashurAmaH	Parshuram
हनुमान	hanumAna	Hanumana
भरतः	bharataH	Bharat
लक्ष्मणः	lakShmaNaH	Lakshman
मनुः	manuH	Manu
जगत्	jagat	jagat
जमदग्निः	jamadAgniH	Jamdagni
मन्वंतरः	manvaMtaraH	manavantara
अक्षरः	akSharaH	akshara
सुमित्रा	sumitraa or sumitrA	Sumitra
मिथिला	mithilA or mithilaa	Mithila

संस्कृत	ITRANS	Indian English
जनक:	janakaH	Janak
इक्ष्वाकु:	ikShvAkuH	Ikshvaku

Note: While ITRANS map is rather accurate, there are two mistakes in the transliteration. The consonant ञ is to be pronounced as 'iyan' and not 'JNa'. The difference is very slight. The conjunct ज्ञ is to be pronounced as 'jyan' as it is a conjunction of ज् and ञ्.

WHY DID I WRITE THIS BOOK?

The inspiration behind studying the life of Shri Rama and Devi Sita in the Ramayana stems purely from my devotion to them. I was very curious to know about their life and time spent in Ayodhya; there is adequate information available about their life in the jungle but not prior to that. While I have heard their stories since I was a child, certain narrations of their *katha* left a lasting impression on my mind.

Growing up, a lot of time was spent at my maternal grandparents' home where I was exposed to the *kathas* or stories of history written in various Hindu scriptures. For Hindus, a *katha* is not just a story, though the word 'story' is used because there is a lack of words to express in the English vocabulary. A *kahani* means a 'story', which could be real or fictional. A *katha* is a real story (with narration) from the history of the Hindus, that they often organise to hear at their homes. A *katha* could be of the Bhagavad Gita, the Ramayana or even *Satya Narayana*, depending on the preference of the person organising it.

Most people alien to Hindu culture would not know that a *katha* involves an elaborate celebration, and it is prepared just like one would a wedding in India. Friends, family and neighbours are invited with due respect and are served food prepared fresh at the venue. Seating as well as sleeping arrangements are made for people coming from other towns. A *katha* includes a *katha vachak* or narrator for whom a seat resembling a throne is constructed and decorated with banana leaves and flowers. Accompanying the *katha vachak* is his entourage, who sing songs and play musical instruments during the narration. This elaborate affair continues for many days.

At one such *katha* organised by my maternal grandparents for the Ramayana, the singer sang songs to depict the *bidai* (farewell) of Devi Sita from Videha after her wedding to Shri Rama. Farewells for brides are an emotional event in real life where her family cries as she departs with the groom. That day, the singer sang with such a sorrowful voice, as if it was his own sister he was saying goodbye to. The singer was so genuinely devoted to Shri Rama and Devi Sita that he could feel the pain of her parents and family as she left for Ayodhya. This brought tears to the eyes of the *katha vachak* and the audience.

Later on, as months passed and I bought *Śrī Rāmacaritamānasa* and started reading it, I observed a similar phenomenon of bursting into tears at various junctures in the book. Reading certain *dohas* (lyrical verses of a poem) from the *Manas* would overwhelm me so much that I could no longer continue reading.

According to Hindu beliefs, on listening to a *katha*, visiting a holy place or reading scriptures, a true devotee often finds himself in tears. It is said that such a person is not only a devotee in his current birth but has also been one in his prior lives. It is also believed that perhaps he had lived along with the deity in one of his previous lives, hence the overwhelming tears.

These experiences became inspirations for me to study the Valmiki Ramayana. I discovered a lot of interesting details in it. The concept behind writing this book stemmed from the desire to share these interesting details of Ayodhya as mentioned by Sage Valmiki, *adi kavi* and creator of the mega epic, Ramayana. Also, there is a lot of misinformation with regards to Valmiki Ramayana and Ayodhya. Accurate descriptions of Ayodhya, as described by Valmiki, were not found in books or blogs either. There was a gap, a vacuum of correct information and representation of life in the Treta Yuga. Therefore, I decided to bridge the gap of understanding between the two yugas—Treta and Kali (the current yuga).

In my opinion, only Valmiki Ramayana is the authoritative source of correct information about the life of Shri Rama and Devi Sita when they lived in Maharaja Dasharatha's Ayodhya. For this reason, it is my primary source of information for *Amazing Ayodhya*. I do not concern myself with the stories of either *Śrī Rāmacaritamānasa* or the Adhyatma Ramayana as authentic sources because they are from a later time than the Ramayanic Era. However, I do respect both these devotional works and often recite the *Sundar Kanda* from *Śrī Rāmacaritamānasa*, written by Tulsidasa.

It is my opinion that the information provided by Sage Valmiki is accurate because he was a contemporary of Shri Rama. Also, if the story of banishment of Devi Sita is true, only he could have had access to the graphic details of the incidents that took place in the lives of Shri Rama and Devi Sita, since Sita was supposed to be living in Sage Valmiki's ashram throughout her banishment.

मंगलाचरण
Manglacharan

माता सीता मत्पिता रामचन्द्रः
रक्षको रामो मत्सखी क्षितिजा ।
सर्वस्वं मे रामचन्द्रो दयालुः
नान्यं जाने नैव जाने न जाने ॥

mAtA sItA matpitA rAmachandra:
rakShako rAmo matsakhI kShitijA |
sarvasvaM me rAmachandro dayAlu:
nAnyaM jAne naiva jAne na jAne ||

My mother is Sita and my father is Rama Chandra.
My protector is Rama and my best friend is Sita.

My everything is merciful Rama.
(I) know not of another, (I really) don't know,
(I really) don't know.

A *manglacharan* is praise or a prayer made to the
worshipper's favourite deity at the start of any
auspicious work. This *manglacharan* is an adaptation
of a *shloka* from the *Rama Raksha Strotra*, wherein I
have tried to convey what I feel about Shri Rama and
Devi Sita. Even though it is impossible to accurately
express the meanings of Sanskrit *shlokas* in English,

I have translated and adapted this one to the best of my knowledge. *Kshitija* is an epithet of Sita which, in Sanskrit, means borne by earth or that which grows in earth. The last line of this *shloka* implies: my everything is Shri Rama and I do not know anything other than Shri Rama.

Introduction

Sung by Luv and Kush, composed by Sage Valmiki, Ramayana has captured the imagination of people across the world since ages. No one growing up in India remains untouched by the story of Shri Rama and Devi Sita.

Every Dussehra, one learns about the victory of Shri Rama over Ravana, the victory of good over evil. Every Deepawali, one hears about how Shri Rama and Devi Sita were welcomed back to Ayodhya. Even today, millions celebrate the festival of Deepavali across the globe.

But amongst the din, only a few pay attention to the fascinating city of Ayodhya. All that is repeated about Ayodhya is that the city was lit up with lamps to welcome its beloved king and queen. But is this all there is to know about Ayodhya?

Sage Valmiki, in his mega epic Ramayana, gives a very interesting and detailed description of the city. The description of Ayodhya, according to Valmiki's Ramayana, is the original resource for all information regarding the ancient city. He writes skillfully about what he sees there.

The sage gives us the history of Ayodhya since the time humans first appeared on earth. He devotes a few chapters of *Bala Kanda* to explain about the city and its fascinating aspects. So if you have ever been curious about Ayodhya or the life of Shri Rama and Devi Sita there, you have come to the right place.

Said Luv and Kush,
'We will sing the song of Ramayana, from the beginning to the end.'

तदिदम् वर्तयिष्यावः सर्वम् निखिलम् आदितः |
धर्म काम अर्थ सहितम् श्रोतव्यम् अनसूयता || १-५-४

tadidam vartayiShyAvaH sarvam nikhilam AditaH |
dharma kAma artha sahitam shrotavyam anasUyatA ||

1-5-4

'Listen without envy or spitefulness to such an epic endowed with the values of dharma, *artha* and *kaama*.'

And they began by giving a fascinating description of Ayodhya.

———————

Part I

ANTIQUITY: ANSWERING THE WHO AND WHEN

In every country, city, district or village, there is
always a first. The first people who settled there or
the first king who established it. Cities, towns and
countries are just like massive trees where one can see
their spread through their leaves and branches, but the
seed that started it all remains hidden underground.
Such is the story of Ayodhya too. Hidden in the dust
of Hindu *itihasa* (history) lies the name of the founder
of Ayodhya.

Sage Valmiki reveals *itihasa* in his mega epic,
mentioning the lineage of the Solar Kings of Bharat
(ancient India) and the story of Shri Rama in much
detail. Valmiki weaves the story of Shri Rama in a
beautifully crafted poem, Ramayana, with thousands of
shlokas distributed into six *kandas*. One of the meanings
of *kanda*, in Sanskrit, is a 'bulb'. From each bulb, there
are multiple creations sprouting forward as *sargas*. Each
sarga contains numerous *shlokas*. Another meaning of
kanda is 'internode'. These are sections of a plant's stem
between two nodes. An example of the former type of
kanda is the bulbuous foot of elephant foot yam, and
the latter type of *kanda* is of the internode of bamboo
or sugarcane.

The answers to the questions raised in this part are
found in *Bala Kanda* and *Yuddha Kanda*.

Who Established Ayodhya?

According to Sage Valmiki, *it was Manu himself who built Ayodhya*. And Manu, after getting Ayodhya built, got it inhabited by people as well. This is written in the 5th *sarga* of *Bala Kanda*.

अयोध्या नाम नगरी तत्र आसीत् लोक विश्रुता |
मनुना मानव इन्द्रेण या पुरी निर्मिता स्वयम् || १-५-६

ayodhyaa naama nagarii tatra aasit loka vishrutaa |
manunaa maanava indreNa yaa purii nirmitaa
svayam || 1-5-6

In this *shloka*, Sage Valmiki states, 'A world-renowned *nagarii* is there in that kingdom (of Kosala), the *purii* of which is personally built by Manu, the foremost ruler of mankind.' *Nagrii* and *purii* will be explained in Part II of this book.

We know that Kosala belonged to Dasharatha, but this *shloka* begs the question: Who was Manu and why does Valmiki call him the foremost ruler of mankind? Why is Manu so important that Valmiki calls him the ruler of mankind?

Who Is Manu?

According to Hindu scriptures, Manu is the icon to who all humankind owe their existence. His importance can be derived from the numerous scriptures he is mentioned in, such as the Mahabharata, the Bhagavad Gita and the *Vishnu Purana*.

Manu is mentioned in the scriptures as '*the first*'. He is the first man. He is the lord amongst men. Manu is the title given to the progenitor of the human species. He is the person who works for the benefit and proliferation of the human race. Therefore, it is Manu who regenerates the world and repopulates it again after a *pralaya* or dissolution/destruction. Each time period of kinship or duration of Manu is called a *manavantara* in Sanskrit. In English, it literally translates to 'the space–time interval of Manu'.

According to Hindu cosmology, there are 14 *manvantaras* in a *kalpa*. Every *manvantara* has a Manu who regenerates it. One *kalpa* of humans is equal to a day of Brahma (the creator). Another *kalpa* is equal to the night of Brahma. In the day *kalpa* of Brahma, the cycle of creation begins and sustains itself. In the night *kalpa* of Brahma, the creation is destroyed and is in a state of rest.

This night and day example of *kalpa* is a simplistic example, but it actually represents a large time interval of creation and destruction of the world as we know it.

Just like day and night come and go for us humans, so do the day and night pass for Brahma, wherein life is created and then destroyed. When talking of creation, we mean earth and all its life forms and not the entire universe, since Brahma's lifespan is supposed to be of 100 days.

According to the Hindu cosmological time cycles, we are currently in the time period of the seventh Manu. Six have come and gone from the total of 14. Each of these *manvantaras* contain 71 maha yugas. One maha yugas contains four yugas. We are currently in the beginning stages of Kali Yuga or the last yuga of one of the maha yugas of the seventh *manvantara*. The elapsed yugas of this maha yugas are Satya Yuga (first), Treta Yuga (second) and Dwapara Yuga (third).

Ramayana was written in the second, Treta Yuga, during which both Valmiki and Lord Vishnu in his seventh incarnation (as Shri Rama) walked the earth. Kali Yuga began with the death of Lord Vishnu's eighth incarnation, Shri Krishna, who gave us the Bhagavad Gita. Shri Krishna is from the Dwapara Yuga.

In each maha yuga of a *manvantara*, a minimum of 10 avatars of the preserver, Lord Vishnu, appear on earth to protect dharma and the righteous. This fact is reiterated by Shri Krishna in the Bhagavad Gita in the following *shlokas* from Chapter 4.

यदा यदा हि धर्मस्य ग्लानिर्भवति भारत |
अभ्युत्थानमधर्मस्य तदात्मानं सृजाम्यहम् || 7||

yadA yadA hi dharmasya glAnirbhavati bhArata |
abhyutthAnamadharmasya tadAtmAnaM
sRRijAmyaham ||7||

It translates to, 'Whenever there is a decline in righteousness and an increase in unrighteousness, O Arjun, at that time I manifest myself on earth.'

परित्राणाय साधूनां विनाशाय च दुष्कृताम् |
धर्मसंस्थापनार्थाय सम्भवामि युगे युगे || 8||

paritrANAya sAdhUnAM vinAshAya cha duShkRRitAm |
dharmasaMsthApanArthAya sambhavAmi yuge yuge | | 8 | |

This shloka means, 'To protect the righteous, to annihilate the wicked, and to reestablish the principles of dharma I appear on this earth, yuga after yuga.'

Shri Rama, born in the lineage of Manu, was the protector of dharma and the righteous in Treta Yuga. The Manu mentioned in the Ramayana is the seventh and the current Manu. He is the great grandson of Brahma. This Manu, however, is not to be confused with Svayambhuva Manu and his wife Satarupa. Svayambhuva Manu is the first Manu and son of Brahma.

According to Hindu cosmology, Brahma had many sons before the first Manu, but they were not interested in the propagation of the human species. It was Svayambhuva Manu and his wife who were the first man and woman to propagate this earth. In Abrahmic religions, they are akin to Adam and Eve. Svayambhuva Manu also authored the code of law for humans titled *Manu Smriti*.

As mentioned before, in ancient times, certain names used to be titles. Manu was such a title given to the progenitor of the human species. Because Svayambhuva was the first progenitor of men on earth, he is the first Manu. Incidentally, the word 'man' is derived from the word *manav* in Sanskrit. The following text explains the etymology of the two words.

The progeny of Manu are called *maanav* in Sanskrit. Spelt as मानव in Sanskrit, the literal meaning of this term is 'children of Manu'. In etymology, the English term 'man' comes from मानव or मान (maanav or maan).

Valmiki addresses him as 'मानवेन्द्र' (maanavendra), which means 'Indra of Men'. 'Indra' in Hindu cosmology is the title of the King of the Gods. In Sanskrit, 'Maanav + Indra' translates to King of Men.

In Sanskrit, the progeny, offspring or people who come from a person are denoted with the suffix 'av' for all words ending with 'u'. Therefore, the progeny of Manu are called *Maanav* (man or humans). The progeny of Danu are called *Daanav*, the progeny or descendents of Yadu are called *Yaadav* and the descendents of Raghu are called *Raaghav*, which is another epithet of Shri Rama. The image below is from the Oxford Dictionary and shows the etymology of man from the name Manu.

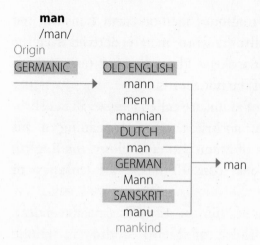

Old English *man (n)*, (plural) menn (noun), *mannian* (verb), of Germanic origin; related to Dutch *man*, German Mann, and Sanskrit *manu* 'mankind'

In Hindu cosmology, another example of a title, apart from that of Manu, is that of Indra. Indra is the King of the Gods who also changes every *manavantara*. There have been various Indras. The Indra of the current *manavantara* is Purandara and it is said that the Indra of the eighth *manavantara* will be King Bali. Another intriguing title or name is Janak. Sita's father is called Janak. It is interesting to note that all kings of the Videha kingdom were called Janak, just like all the progenitors of humans (of every *kalpa*) are called Manu. 'Janak' in Sanskrit means 'father'.

While Manu and Indra are both titles, Janak seems to be a titular name of the kings in the same lineage. It was tradition to name each successive king Janak in the Videha kingdom. Fascinatingly, some of these ancient traditions made their way to the modern era too. Several kings of France practised the tradition of naming all their rulers 'Louis'.

Coming back to Manu, the Manu mentioned in the Ramayana is called 'Vaivasvata Manu'. He is called Vaivasvata because he is the son of the Sun God, Vivasvan. In Sanskrit, the meaning of Vaivasvata is that which belongs to Vivasvan (like an offspring).

The *Vishnu Purana* further mentions that Vaivasvata Manu, his family and the *saptrishis* (seven sages), along with the holy books of the Hindus, the Vedas, were saved from the great flood by the Matsya Avatar, the first avatar of Lord Vishnu. According to the *Vishnu Purana*, the seven sages of Vaivasvata *manavantara* are Kashyapa, Bhardwaja, Atri, Vashishtha, Gautama, Jamdagni and Vishwamitra. Since Vaivasvata manages to save humans and later propagates the earth, Lord Vishnu then makes him the ruler of this *manvantara* and bestows upon him the title of Manu. In Abrahmic religions, Vaivasvata Manu would be akin to Noah, who also saves mankind and land animals from extinction during the great flood.

The 'great flood' from which Vaivasvata Manu saves humans is called *pralaya* in Sanskrit. *Pralaya* refers to the end of all existing life forms (on earth). As mentioned previously, Vaivasvata Manu comes after six Manus have come and gone, making us the *maanav* of the seventh *manvantara*. Since six *manvantaras* have elapsed from the total of 14, a total of six *pralayas* have passed. There are seven more Manus to go before the current *kalpa* of *Shveta Varaha* or *kalpa* of White Boar ends.

The above image depicts Vaivasvata Manu and his family and *saptarishis* being led by Lord Vishnu in his Matsya Avatar. This image has been sourced from a version of Valmiki's Ramayana by Ram Narayan Dutt Shastri (Gita Press, Gorakhpur), and published on Wikipedia. 'Matsya' in Sanskrit means 'fish', and what better being could survive *pralaya* than a massive fish! The fish avatar or the Matsya Avatar of Lord Vishnu is the first avatar of this *manvantara* and appeared in Satya Yuga.

It is pertinent to note that Manu had 10 children. Two of his children, Ila and Ikshvaku, are the progenitors of the Lunar and Solar dynasties respectively. The descendants of the Solar dynasty are called Suryavanshi and those of the Lunar dynasty are called Chandravanshi. The progenitor of the Solar dynasty is the Sun God, Vivasvan, and the progenitor of the Lunar dynasty is Moon God Chandra. Shri Rama, the seventh avatar of

Vishnu, is from the Solar dynasty and is the scion of Ikshvaku. Shri Krishna, the eighth avatar of Vishnu, is from the Lunar dynasty and is a descendant of Ila.

We can also gauge Manu's importance by the fact that his name is invoked before any puja or *homa* (fire prayer) begins. The invocation of his name is a part of *Sankalpa Mantra*, which is a resolve taken for something positive before embarking on any kind of worship. The resolve underlines the reason for that particular worship. No worship—puja, chanting, meditation, *homa*—is ever started without a resolve. A *Sankalpa Mantra* includes, amongst other things, a geolocation pin, a space–time location and a lineage description of oneself. An example of a *Sankalpa Mantra* is given below with the *Vaivasvata-Manvantara* highlighted.

ॐ विष्णुर्विष्णुर्विष्णुः । ॐ श्रीमन्द्भगवतो महापुरुषस्य
विष्णोराज्ञया प्रवर्तमानस्य ब्रह्मणो द्वितीयेपरार्द्धे
श्रीश्वेतवाराहकल्पे वैवस्वतमन्वन्तरे अष्टाविंशतितमे कलियुगे
कलिप्रथमचरणे भूर्लोके जम्बूद्विपे भारतवर्षे भरतखण्डे
आर्यावर्तैं कंतर्गत ....तीरे .... क्षेत्रे ....
मण्डलान्तरगते .... नाम्निनगरे (ग्रामे वा) ....
देवब्राह्मणानां सन्निधौ श्रीमन्नृपतिवीरविक्रमादित्यसमयतः ....
संख्या - परिमिते प्रवर्त्तमानसंवत्सरे नामसंवत्सरे, रवि...........
अयने, ... ऋतौ, ... मासे, ... पक्षे, ... तिथौ,
.... वासरे, ... नक्षत्रे, ... योगे, ... करणे,
.... राशिस्थिते चन्द्रे, ... राशिस्थितेश्रीसूर्ये, ...
देवगुरौ शेषेषु ग्रहेषु यथायथा राशिस्थानस्थितेषु एवं
ग्रहगुणविशेषणविशिष्टायां शुभपुण्यतिथौ .... गोत्र
उत्पन्नोहम् ..... नामाहम् मङ्गलकार्यं .... पूजनम् / दानम् /
होमम् अहं करिष्ये।

In the Bhagavad Gita, Shri Krishna talks about Manu in the fourth chapter. This chapter is called *Jyana Yoga* (Yoga of True Knowledge) and in it Lord Krishna reveals how true spiritual knowledge is received by disciplic succession. In the first *shloka* of the fourth chapter, Shri Krishna clearly mentions that he taught the eternal science of yoga to the Sun God Vivasvan. Vivasvan passed it on to his son Manu, who in turn, did the same to Ikshvaku. The *shloka* is mentioned below with *Vivasvan* highlighted.

श्रीभगवानुवाच |
इमं <u>विवस्वते</u> योगं प्रोक्तवानहमव्ययम् |
विवस्वान्मनवे प्राह मनुरिक्ष्वाकवेऽब्रवीत् || 1||

shrIbhagavAn uvAcha |
imaM <u>vivasvate</u> yogaM proktavAnahamavyayam |
vivasvAnmanave prAha manurikShvAkave.abravt ||1||

Vivasvan, Manu and Ikshvaku received knowledge by disciplic succession, where someone who is a perfect authority on a particular subject passes it down to another who wishes to learn it. All three of them are named by Shri Krishna as they are revered in Dwapara Yuga too, for knowing the eternal science of yoga.

Now that we have understood the importance of Manu and the lineage of the Solar dynasty, the antiquity of Ayodhya needs to be ascertained. In the next chapter, we will discover when Ayodhya was established.

When Was Ayodhya Established?

Shedding light on the importance and antiquity of Manu also brings the ancient origins of Ayodhya to focus. Since Manu, the king amongst humans, is the first man, Ayodhya is as old as humankind itself. Manu established Ayodhya sometime after the *pralaya* in Satya Yuga and Ayodhya has been continuously inhabited ever since. Therefore, Hindus revere Ayodhya as the cradle of human civilisation and it has always been an important place, even before the birth of Shri Rama. Since the birth of Shri Rama in Treta Yuga, it became a place of supreme importance to Hindus all over the world.

An interesting fact about the unbroken link of the Solar dynasty from Satya Yuga to Treta Yuga, from the time of Manu to Shri Rama, is mentioned in Valmiki Ramayana. This is an item that was handed over to Lord Rama. Can you guess what it is?

Unbroken Link of the Solar Dynasty from Satya Yuga to Treta Yuga

According to Sage Valmiki, Manu is not only important to the Hindu history but also to Shri Rama. Towards the end of Valmiki Ramayana, after Shri Rama wins the war against Ravana and comes back to Ayodhya, Shri Rama is crowned with an antique crown during his *pattabhishekam* or coronation ceremony.

That antique crown was fashioned and crafted by Brahma himself. Amazingly, in the Ramayana, the crown has been described as 'ancient'. If for us the Ramayana is ancient today, the crown being older than that is rather intriguing. It is this ancient crown that serves as the unbroken link of the Solar dynasty from Satya Yuga to Treta Yuga.

In the *Yuddha Kanda,* where the *pattabhishekam* of Lord Rama is being conducted, Valmiki describes the following, 'With which *kirii Tam* crown, long ago, Manu the emperor was adorned while he was consecrated and with which the kings that followed in his line were successively adorned while they were coronated, that crown studded with precious jewels, fashioned by Brahma at the beginning of creation and dazzling with splendour, kept according to practice on a throne adorned with many kinds of precious stones in the council hall, studded with gold, graced with abundant riches, decorated and shiningly made with the most charming jewels of various kinds, and thereafter Rama was duly adorned by that crown as well as jewels by the great-souled Vasishta and other priests officiating at the coronation ceremony.' You can find the Sanskrit version below:

ब्रह्मणा निर्मितं पूर्वं किरीटं रत्नशोभितम् || ६-१२८-६४
अभिषिक्तः पुरा येन मनुस्तं दीप्ततेजसम् |
तस्यान्ववाये राजानः क्रमाद्येनाभिषेचिताः || ६-१२८-६५
सभायां हेमक्लुप्तायां शोभितायां महाधनैः |
रत्नैर्नानाविधैश्चैव चित्रितायां सुशोभनैः || ६-१२८-६६
नानारत्नमये पीठे कल्पयित्वा यथाविधि |
किरीटेन ततः पश्चाद्वसिष्ठेन महात्मना || ६-१२८-६७
ऋत्विग्भिर्भूषणैश्चैव समयोक्ष्यत राघवः |

brahmaNaa nirmitam puurvam kiriiTam
ratnashobhitam || 6-128-64
abhiShiktaH puraa yena manuH tam diipta tejassam |
tasya anvavaaye raajaanaH kramedyenaa
abhiShechitaaH || 6-128-65
sabhaayaam hemakluptaayaam shobhitaayaam
mahaadhanaiH |
ratnaiH naanaavidhaiH chitritaayaam sushobhanaiH
|| 6-128-66
naanaaratnamaye piiThe kalpayitvaa yathaa vidhi |
kiriiTena tataH pashchaat vasiShTena mahaatmanaa
|| 6-128-67
R^itvigbhiH bhuuShaNaishchaiv samayokShyata
raaghavaH |

To elucidate upon the coronation ceremony, an image of
an elaborate crown from ancient times is shown below.
This image is just to illustrate the elaborate design of
a bejewelled crown in ancient times, so that the reader
can get a visual reference. This crown is mentioned in
the book *The Architecture of Manasara*. Manasara wrote
a treatise on *Shilpa Shastra* and *Vastu Shastra*. The
crown image given here is that of a *mauli* crown though
the one that belonged to Manu was called a *kiriiT*. The
crowns *mauili* and *kiriiT* differ in shape, but are both
bejewelled and elaborately detailed.

It is wonderful to observe how Valmiki cleverly stitches the long story of Ayodhya from *Bala Kanda* to *Yudha Kanda*. He starts with the story of the inception of Ayodhya by Manu and ends it with the handing over of Kosala's throne in Ayodhya to Lord Rama, thereby maintaining the continuity and passing down of Manu's enchanting gem-studded, gold crown from generation to generation.

Now that we have established the antiquity of Ayodhya, we will proceed to know more about the location of Ayodhya and Kosala.

Part II

'LOCATION. LOCATION. LOCATION': ANSWERING THE WHERE AND WHAT

Before we get the exact coordinates of Ayodhya, it is important to know what Ayodhya was in those days because it is different from what the city is today. The confusion in the minds of people with regards to the Ayodhya of Treta Yuga will be addressed here.

What Was Ayodhya?

A city? An empire? A village?

People are often confused about whether Ayodhya of the Ramayanic Era was a city, a country, an empire or a village. Sometimes, people have wrongly referred to Ayodhya as a kingdom. Sage Valmiki, however, clearly defines Ayodhya as a *nagarii*.

What Is a *Nagarii*?

Nagara and *nagarii* are both Sanskrit words that mean district. They are often wrongly used to mean a city. This mistake in translation has been made by both commentators and translators. The concept of district has remained almost the same from ancient times till today.

A district normally includes:

Rural areas or villages, for farming and cultivation;

Urban area or a city; and sometimes,

A capital district or a *purii*.

A district in Sanskrit is referred to in all three genders, namely *nagara* (masculine), *nagarii* (feminine) and *nagaram* (neutral). This should not be confusing as Valmiki keeps shifting between these words to suit his narrative and to create rhyming syllables of *shlokas*. In Sanskrit grammar, there are three genders and gender classification is not based on the nature of objects, whether they are animate or inanimate. Gender classification follows a set of rules that are deduced from dictionaries, Panini's grammar books and scriptures. Another example is the word 'shore' or 'bank', which in Sanskrit has three genders too, namely *taTaH* (masculine), *taTii* (feminine) and *taTam* (neutral).

तटः तटी तटम्

Sometimes, the difference in genders can indicate sizes too, but not always. In the above example, a *taTaH* would be slightly bigger than a *taTii* and a *taTii* would be slightly bigger than *taTam*. But this is not always the case. One has to bear in mind the context when deriving a difference in size from the gender of the word.

In the Ramayana, Sage Valmiki uses the word *purii*, apart from *nagara*, to describe Ayodhya when it was established by Manu. *Nagarii* and *purii*, both have different meanings in Sanskrit and Hindi.

In the first part of the sixth *shloka* of *sarga* 5, *Bala Kanda*, a clear mention of the word *nagarii* used in the context of Ayodhya—*ayodhyaa naama nagarii loka vishrutaa*, which means 'the *nagarii* by the name of Ayodhya is famous in the world'.

In the second part, Sage Valmiki says that it was Manu himself who personally established this *purii*. The *shloka* is given below in Roman script.

ayodhyaa naama nagarii tatra aasit loka vishrutaa |
manunaa maanava indreNa yaa purii svayam
nirmitaa || 1-5-6

Here, Valmiki also specifies that this district is famous in the world. In later *shlokas*, to validate the same, he names various countries from where people came to Ayodhya to trade. Since Ayodhya was an international trading capital, many types of people and foreigners were settled there too.

But why does Valmiki use both *nagarii* and *purii* in the same *shloka* to describe Ayodhya? And what is the difference between the two? What is he trying to imply in the *shloka*?

The inability to decipher the difference between a *nagarii* and a *purii*, followed by its incorrect translation, is the reason behind the confusion with regards to Ayodhya either being a city, an empire or a village. This difference will be made clear in the next sub-chapter.

Is There a Difference between a *Nagara* and a *Purii*?

In Sanskrit, *nagara* is described as being bigger than a village, town or city. It is a district where many people belonging to various tribes and different professions stay. A district can have both urban and rural areas within it. The word *nagarii* means the same as *nagara*, which comprises 'the urban and suburban plus rural and rustic areas inside the district'. Both *nagara* and *nagarii* are used interchangeably, as described earlier, based on the rules of Sanskrit grammar.

Purii is a feminine word and so are *pura*, *pur* and *puraa*. They are all synonymous. In Hindi, *pur* is described as a city where lots of people come and go for work.

So *pur* is more like a city and *purii* is used synonymously in the Ramayana.

In Sanskrit dictionaries, *purii* has various meanings like constellation, *lok* (other worlds), a villa, a mansion and even a human body. This can confuse any reader or researcher. Things can get worse if one uses certain websites to find the differences in the meaning of the two. One website is quite clear that a *pur* is 'a sound a cat makes' and a *puri* is a 'deep-fried, round type of unleavened bread from India and Pakistan'. Well, I didn't know how to react to that. At this point in my research, I did not know whether I wanted to laugh or cry.

In Sanskrit, *purii* also means a centre where important people stay, especially those who have a say in the matters of running the kingdom, including the king and his men. In a democratic country, a *purii* would translate to where the prime minister and his cabinet ministers reside as well as where diplomats are lodged. Some may even refer to *purii* as a capital district where the seat of the country's government and important administrative divisions are located. A perfect example of it would be Chanakyapuri in New Delhi, India.

Chanakyapuri in New Delhi is named after Chanakya or Kautilya, who was the most important advisor and mentor of the Mauryan Emperor Chandragupta. It is Chanakya who had put Chandragupta on the throne and established the Mauryan Empire. In today's Chanakyapuri, both politicians and civil servants of the Government of India reside. It also houses various diplomatic mission headquarters in the country and it is located near the prime minister's residence.

The concept of a *purii* is based on the fact that for a king, all his men should be available to him whenever he needs them. To fulfil this purpose, it was important that they all lived close to the ruler, and in case of emergencies, could be summoned at the shortest notice.

It is important to note the differences between *nagarii* and *purii* because Valmiki uses both words to convey the vastness and multifarious design of Ayodhya. In ancient times, it was not always necessary that a *nagarii* would also be a *purii* or vice versa. However, Ayodhya was a *nagarii* with a *purii* in it, implying that the urban region of the district (the city) had a *purii* in the middle of it. This implies that Ayodhya *nagarii* (district) had Ayodhya *purii* (administrative capital centre) within its boundaries. Both *nagarii* and *purii* were addressed by the same name—Ayodhya.

In many cases in India even today, just like in the past, the urban part of the district (the city) and the district have the same name. Examples from Kali Yuga (today) are Meerut, Bareily and Amritsar. All of them have the same name for the city as well as the district. These cities do not contain the administrative capital centres of the state though they may contain administrative centres for their respective districts, within their boundaries.

There could be more than one city in a district and in the past, each *nagara* has at least one urban region. A *purii* is the administrative centre in the urban area (the city) of the *nagara*. Not all *nagaras* had a capital administrative area and the king's residence though a local administrative area like a municipality could exist in its city.

To explain this using Delhi's example, prior to January 1997, there was only one district for the whole of Delhi with its district headquarters at Tis Hazari. The district of Delhi also contained within it Chanakyapuri, which is the administrative capital of the country, as it houses all the important people of the country. Both Tis Hazari and Chanakyapuri are headquarters. One is for the district itself and the other is for the country.

Today, the *purii* of Delhi does not have the same name as the district of Delhi, but in ancient times, the *purii* and district had the same name. Ayodhya would be the prime example from the Treta Yuga, where the *purii* and the *nagarii* had the same name but they were distinct from one another. Their distinction in the Ramayana is made out only by the mention of *nagarii* and *purii* and not by the name Ayodhya.

Just like in olden days, even today the distinction between *nagara* and *pur* is maintained in India. Examples of *pur* are Nagpur, Kanpur and Jaunpur. And examples of *nagara* are Itanagar, Srinagar and Tatanagar. Unfortunately, as towns have grown and some cities have shrunk with the passage of time, the meaning of *nagara* and *pur* have become homogenous in the vocabulary of the younger generation. But unlike the olden days, these *purs* are neither the capitals nor do they contain the capital administrative centre.

Interestingly, the word *naagar* in Sanskrit does not describe either a city or district but people. This word is derived from the word *nagara*. The word *naagar* implies 'sophistication' or 'sophisticated' when used for people. In Sanskrit, this word means 'that which belongs to a *nagara*'. It is fair to assume that people of the district were considered to be more sophisticated than those of the jungle areas or those who lived outside the embankments of the *nagara*.

Another interesting word derived from *nagara* is the word *naagrik*, which means a citizen. At present, the concept of *naagrik* has broadened and implies a citizen of a country. In the past, it may have applied to the people of a district, as most populations used to live within the four walls of the strongholds. A district, in earlier times, was enveloped within a fortress or a stronghold with a high wall surrounding it. Today, even though our borders are on the edges of our country and not on the edges of the districts, the essence of *naagrik* remains the same—citizens.

Based on the information discussed above, we can critically re-examine the description given by Valmiki, so that the difference becomes clearer. In the *Bala Kanda, sarga* 5, Valmiki uses the word *purii* in his *shloka* to define and emphasise that the *purii* (of Ayodhya) was built by Manu.

In the same *shloka*, Valmiki also says that the city is famous in the whole world. That is because it has been established by Manu and continuously ruled by his Suryavanshi successors for a long, long time, from Satya Yuga to Treta Yuga. Before the birth of Shri Rama, it was a powerful place ruled by powerful kings and a centre of trade too.

An English translation of the following *shloka* is: 'A world-renowned *nagarii* is there in that kingdom (of Kosala), the *purii* of which is personally built by Manu, the foremost ruler of mankind.'

अयोध्या नाम नगरी तत्र आसीत् लोक विश्रुता |
मनुना मानव इन्द्रेण या पुरी निर्मिता स्वयम् || १-५-६

ayodhyaa naama nagarii tatra aasit loka vishrutaa |
manunaa maanava indreNa yaa purii nirmitaa
svayam || 1-5-6

In three *shlokas* after the one above in the same *sarga*
5, Sage Valmiki makes apparent the difference between
purii and *nagara* when he mentions that Dasharatha
had contributed by expanding the city. The current size
(at the time of writing Ramayana) was attributed to
Maharaja Dasharatha, Shri Rama's father.

ताम् तु राजा दशरथो महाराष्ट्र विवर्धनः |
पुरीम् आवासयामास दिवि देवपतिः यथा || १-५-९

taam tu raajaa dasharathaH mahaa raaSTra
vivardhanaH |
puriim aavaasayaamaasa divi deva patiH yathaa ||
1-5-9

The above *shloka* translates to: 'As an improver of
the great kingdom Dasharatha, the king, made her
(Ayodhya) his abode, as Indra made heavens his abode.'
The Sanskrit phrase *mahaa raaSTra vivardhanaH* used
in the *shloka* implies that he restructured and added
more states to his empire. The English word 'improver'
in this context is synonymous with expansion of the
district to incorporate the burgeoning population that
lived there.

The Sanskrit word *aavaasayaamaasa* is also used for resettling. This means that the kingdom was doing well under the king and hordes of people were living there. As Dasharatha expanded the empire, he resettled the population too—in the great district (Ayodhya), which resembled heaven. I will talk about the population in Part III of the book. But before that, let's decode the location of Ayodhya.

As of now, many efforts to reclaim the lost glory of Ayodhya have been undertaken by the current Chief Minister Yogi Adityanath. When the process of writing this book started in 2017, Ayodhya was a city in the district of Faizabad in the northern and most populous state of India, Uttar Pradesh. On 6 November 2018, the Uttar Pradesh cabinet approved renaming of Faizabad district as Ayodhya, and shifting the administrative headquarters of the district to Ayodhya city.

6

Where Was Ayodhya Located?

Most of us know that Ayodhya is located on the banks of Sarayu River. Sage Valmiki also confirms the same. In the Ramayana, he adds that Ayodhya is a part of a kingdom called Kosala. Valmiki declares, 'Ayodhya is the capital of Kosala.'

The description given in Sanskrit by Valmiki about the location of both Kosala and Ayodhya are given in two simultaneous *shlokas*:

> *kosalaH naama muditaH sphiitaH janapadaH*
> *mahaan |*
> *niviSTaH sarayuu tiire prabhuuta dhana*
> *dhaanyavaan ||* 1-5-5

> *ayodhyaa naama nagarii tatra aasit loka vishrutaa |*
> *manunaa maanava indreNa yaa purii svayam*
> *nirmitaa ||* 1-5-6

The translation of the two *shlokas* states: 'A great empire named Kosala, a joyous and a vast one well flourishing with monies and cereals, is snugly situated on the riverbanks of Sarayu. A world-renowned district, Ayodhya, is there in that empire, the *purii* of which is personally built by Manu, the foremost ruler of mankind.' The Sanskrit images of the *shlokas* have been shared in this and the previous chapter.

Therefore, we can confirm from the *shlokas* that ancient Ayodhya, too, was on the banks of Sarayu, just as Kosala. In the picture below, the location of Sarayu and Ayodhya is depicted clearly. The image of Ayodhya is as per Google Maps, June 2017. Now that Ayodhya has been decoded, in the next chapter we will discuss where the empire of Kosala is located.

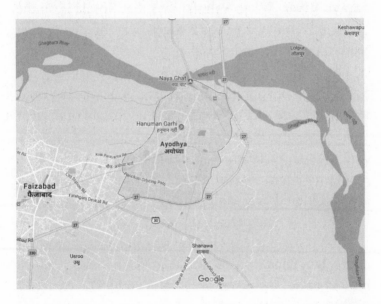

7

Where Was Kosala?

We now know the exact location of Ayodhya and know that Kosala, too, was around the banks of Sarayu River. When Valmiki says that Kosala is on the banks of Sarayu, he uses a poetic way of saying that Sarayu flows through Kosala.

There might have been other rivers in Kosala too, but Sarayu was of supreme importance, as it was the river that fed the district of Ayodhya. The Kosala of ancient India was abundant in *dhana* and *dhaanya* (money and grains) as mentioned in *shloka* 5 by Valmiki—*prabhuuta dhana dhaanyavaan*. Both money and grain are considered as wealth in the Hindu culture and can be stored for long periods of time.

Money for ancient Hindus was not just a piece of paper but consisted of actual gold and silver coins, minted under the order of the monarch. The currency itself was valuable, unlike today, where it only carries an implied value and no real value.

The Sanskrit word for grains is *dhaanya*. *Dhaanya* refers to grain that is cultivated and has a sheath or shell, which forms a covering around it in order to protect it. Perishable food items like vegetables are not included in *dhaanya*. Wheat, rice and barley are examples of *dhaanya*. To grow wealth, that is, grains, a continuous flow of water is required. The fact that Ayodhya was abundant in *dhaanya* implies that she had a continuous supply of fresh water as well as fertile soil.

Here, it is important to make the connection between wealth and water. It is because of this reason that most ancient countries or civilisations across the world were settled around rivers. Examples of two such prosperous Hindu civilisations whose remains have been excavated are the Saraswati River and Indus River civilisations. Below is an image of India during the Ramayanic Era sourced from mahanbharat. net, which shows the rivers as well as the kingdoms surrounding them.

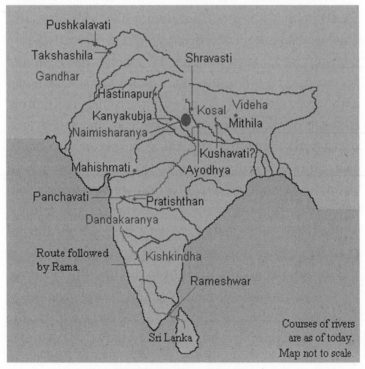

Bharat during Ramayanic Time

Here, the kingdoms during the time of Valmiki's
Ramayana along with Kosala and Ayodhya are clearly
marked, and so is the path taken by Lord Rama to reach
Sri Lanka. One can clearly see that the area of Kosala
extended on both sides of the Sarayu River.

In the book *Arthashastra*, Kautilya states clearly that
a kingdom should have strongholds in all four corners.
In Chapter 3 of the *Arthashastra* titled 'Construction of
Forts', under the duties of government superintendents,
Kautilya instructs that: 'On all the four quarters of the
boundaries of the kingdom, defensive fortifications
against an enemy in war shall be constructed on
grounds naturally best fitted for the purpose: a water-
fortification (*audaka*), such as an island in the midst
of a river or a plain surrounded by low ground; a
mountainous fortification (*paarvata*), such as a rocky
tract or a cave; a desert (*dhaanvana*), such as a wild tract
devoid of water and overgrown with thickets growing
in barren soil; or a forest fortification (*vanadurga*), full
of wagtail (*khajana*), water and thickets. Of these, water
and mountain fortifications are best suited to defend
populous centres, and desert and forest fortifications
are habitations in wilderness (*ataviisthaana*).'

Kautilya, who walked the earth probably around
the 2nd century BCE, himself derives his wisdom from
the sages before his yuga; he also mentions their names
in his book. Such 'kingdom planning' was common in
those days. Going by the insights of Kautilya and the
sages before him, it is clear that Ayodhya was perhaps
on one corner of Kosala, with Sarayu River on its north.
And that there would have been many other districts of

Kosala that are not mentioned in as much graphic detail as Ayodhya.

Considering that Ayodhya is only a part of the Kosala Kingdom, how big was Kosala in the Treta Yuga?

———

8

How Big Was Kosala?

Since the description of Ayodhya is incomplete without a proper introduction to Kosala, an attempt to define it has been undertaken in this book. Various small details of Kosala are spread across the Ramayana. Sage Valmiki says Kosala is a *mahaan janpada*.

Janpada in Sanskrit/Hindi means a kingdom or a country. A *mahaan janpada* in this *shloka* would translate to a grand or vast kingdom, meaning an empire. The following line from the Ramayana elucidates the same in Sanskrit: *kosalaH naama muditaH sphiitaH janapadaH mahaan*.

कोसलो नाम मुदितः स्फीतो जनपदो महान् ।
निविष्ट सरयू तीरे प्रभूत धन धान्यवान् ॥ १-५-५

kosalaH naama muditaH sphiitaH janapadaH mahaan |
niviSTaH sarayuu tiire prabhuuta dhana
dhaanyavaan || 1-5-5

A *mahaan janpad* is an empire and not just a kingdom even though one finds the word 'kingdom' in most translations. In the next chapter, we will find out why Kosala is an empire and not a kingdom. Also, a clear answer to the vastness of Kosala is mentioned in a later chapter—in the form of a dialogue between Emperor Dasharatha and Empress Kaikeyi. Empress Kaikeyi was the second empress of Dasharatha; Kaushalya and Sumitra were the first and third respectively.

9

Was Kosala a Kingdom or an Empire?

In the English language, there is a difference between a 'kingdom' and an 'empire'. An empire encompasses several states and countries, which are ruled by a single emperor or empress. On the other hand, a kingdom is a country that is ruled by a king or a queen.

This distinction between the two is somewhat blurred in Indian languages today. Various English translations of the Ramayana do not clearly differentiate while translating either. A kingdom and an empire are almost used synonymously in Indian languages. Poets, including Valmiki, use these words interchangeably in order to fit syllables to suit particular metres of poetry.

However, Sage Valmiki clearly differentiates between a kingdom and an empire by stating in *shloka* 14 of *sarga* 5, *Bala Kanda—saamanta raaja sanghaiH cha bali karmabhiH aavR^itam*. This translates to, 'Large groups of provincial kings (*saamanta raaja)* crowd Ayodhya to pay their taxes.' The corresponding *shloka* is given below.

सामंत राज सन्चैः च बलि कर्मभिः आवृतम् ।
नाना देश निवासैः च वणिग्भिः उपशोभिताम् ॥ १-५-१४

saamanta raaja sanghaiH cha bali karmabhiH
aavR^itam |
naa naa desha nivaasaiH cha vaNikbhiH upa
shobhtaam || 1-5-14

In Sanskrit, *saamanta raaja* also translates to rulers of neighbouring states, similar to the English term 'provincial kings'. A ruler will pay tax to another king only if he is under the dominion of that powerful king or an emperor. Thus, Valmiki makes it clear that Kosala was an empire. There is no ambiguity in his words.

The English term 'province' is derived from the ancient Roman word *provincia*. In the vast Roman Empire, stretching from the United Kingdom to territories throughout Europe, North Africa and the Middle East, a *provincia* was a major territorial and administrative unit of its possessions outside of Italy.

The Roman Empire, in the history of the Western civilisation, is one of the largest empires. Both the size of the Roman Empire and their expansionist ideology is expressed in the Latin phrase *imperium sine fine*, which means 'empire without end'. The ideology behind this phrase implied that neither time nor space limited the Roman Empire.

In such a vast empire, tax collection must have been a herculean task. It's no wonder they divided the empire beyond the boundaries of Italy into *provincia*. Since those ancient times, the term 'province' has been adopted by many countries.

The Hindu system of 'provinces' was called *saamanta*, a concept that predates the Roman Empire. The Hindu civilisation saw many empires come and go like the Magdha, the Pandyan and the Gandhara Empires. Many Hindu empires (similar to the Roman Empire) existed simultaneously in ancient times much preceeding the epoch of the Romans. Each Hindu empire's emperor had numerous smaller provincial kings under his dominion. The Kosala Empire was one such under the Emperor Dasharatha.

The clever Sage Valmiki also clarifies the extent of the Kosala Empire, which is discussed in the next chapter. It will also provide deeper clarity about Kosala Empire with reference to the kings under Emperor Dasharatha's dominion. Can you guess how many kings there were?

———

10

How Many Kings Were under Dasharatha's Dominion?

We have ascertained that an empire encompasses several states and countries ruled by a single emperor or empress. Emperor Dasharatha had many provincial kings who came and paid taxes in Ayodhya. In *shloka* 28 (second part), *sarga* 6 of *Bala Kanda*, the great Sage Valmiki says:

ताम् सत्य नामाम् दृढ तोरण अर्गलाम्
गृहैः विचित्रैः उपशोभिताम् शिवाम् |
पुरीम् अयोध्याम् नृ सहस्र संकुलाम्
शशास वै शक्र समो महीपतिः || १-६-२८

puriim ayodhyaam nR^i sahastra sankulaam |
shashaasa vai shakra samaH mahiipatiH || 1-6-28

The *shloka* translates to, 'and full with thousands of provincial kings too, and the *mahiipatiH* (lord of earth), a coequal of Indra, indeed ruled that capital which is true to its name'.

The word *sahastra* means a thousand in Sanskrit. A 1,000 provincial kings are in Ayodhya *purii*, says Valmiki. Dasharatha is also called *mahiipatiH* and *shakra samaH. MahiipatiH* means the lord of the earth. And, this lord of the earth is also *shakra samaH*, which means someone who is equal to Indra, the lord of heavens. This comparison of Dasharatha to Indra is done to impress upon his status as an emperor.

Indra, in Hindu cosmology, is the king amongst gods in heaven. All the gods reside in a place called *svarga* which has been loosely translated to 'heaven' in English. *Svarga* is a plane of existence higher than that of the humans where more evolved beings reside. These beings are called deva, devi and *devata*, etc., which are translated to gods and goddesses.

Gods and goddesses in Hindu cosmology are not independent, random players causing havoc but instead, work in tandem to help mankind and all living entities though they may sometimes cause mischief to test certain human beings and know their potential. They have a selected king or a president called Indra, which is a title. Indra is above all other Gods in position but beneath the trinity of Brahma, the creator, Vishnu, the preserver and Shiva, the destroyer. This is one reason why Dasharatha is compared to Indra.

In some places, this *shloka* has been mistranslated to 'thousands of people' rather than 'thousands of provincial kings'. The actual meaning of the *shloka* only makes sense with 'thousands of provincial kings' (in Ayodhya) because there would be no reason to compare him to Indra otherwise. A thousand provincial kings is also in sync with the mention of thousands of *saamanta raaja* described in the previous chapter.

Also, in *shloka* 27 prior to *shloka* 28 discussed above, Valmiki alludes to Emperor Dasharatha's reign over the various kingdoms of his empire. This *shloka* is a simile for the emperor and his empire.

ताम् पुरीम् स महातेजा राजा दशरथो महान् |
शशास शमितः अमित्रो नक्षत्राणीव चन्द्रमाः ||१-६-२७

taam puriim sa maha tejaaH raaja dasharathaH mahaan |
sashaasa shamitaH amitraH nakshatraaNi iva
chandramaaH | | 1-6-27

It translates to, 'In that city (Ayodhya) the great resplendent and admirable king Dasharatha resided, he ruled the world from that city with silenced enemies, like the moon governing the constellations.' The Sanskrit word *shamitaH amitraH* means 'silenced, appeased, allayed, destroyed or vanquished' those who are 'not friends'. Constellations are made up of numerous stars, and the most resplendent of all the visible things in the sky is the moon.

Poets are clever, but Valmiki is a genius with words. He follows many rules of poetry—not to use the same words repeatedly and to use flowery language to express even the mundane. This *shloka*, again, makes it more than obvious that Dasharatha had innumerable kings under his dominion. Those who were not his friends were either silenced or appeased or conquered and brought under the dominion of Kosala. Emperor Dasharatha was unparalleled amongst the kings on earth, just like the moon is in the sky. It is the brightest object in the sky, far surpassing the brightness of the stars and constellations.

In *shloka* 5, *sarga* 5, Valmiki says: *kosalaH naama muditaH sphiitaH janapadaH mahaan*. And in the *shloka* above of *sarga 6*, Valmiki says: *raaja dasharathaH mahaan*. It is obvious that a *mahaan janapada* like that of Kosala will have a *mahaan* raja or a maharaja.

The *Vedic Index of Names and Subjects* defines a maharaja as a 'great king' and the same is frequently referred to in the Brahmanas too. In Sanskrit dictionaries, a maharaja means a great king and a supreme sovereign. This is opposed to a mere prince who would just be given the title of a 'king' or a *rajan*.

Usually, according to the Hindus, a king was called a maharaja if he had a thousand kings under his dominion. This is the relevance of the number 'thousand' in the above *shlokas*. This dominion over so many kings is another reason why Dasharatha is compared to Indra.

To sum it up, one can clearly gauge that there were a minimum of a thousand kings under his dominion. Though the Ramayana does not make it very clear how many times over did he become a maharaja, meaning, how many thousand kingdoms he repeatedly acquired under his dominion, considering he was rather old and had regularly participated in the *Ashvamedha Yagya*.

The *Ashvamedha Yagya* was an act by the Hindu emperors to prove their imperial sovereignty over neighbouring, provincial and new kingdoms or territories. Under this *yagya* (fire ritual), a king's horse and a portion of his warriors would wander over a period of time. The horse, mostly white in colour, was free to traverse as it pleased in various territories.

Stopping the horse anywhere was tantamount to challenging the sovereign authority of the emperor and an invitation to battle. The person challenging the movement of the horse would first have to battle with the portion of the travelling warriors and then the army of the emperor. If the horse, after the stipulated time (a year), travelled back to the emperor unchallenged, then he would be declared an undisputed sovereign. It is worth mentioning here that ordinary kings could not participate in the *Ashvamedha Yagya*, and it was only to be performed by powerful Hindu maharajas.

The Sanskrit words *maha* and *mahaan* are similar. While both mean 'great', *maha* also means large in number. We have established the maharaja status of Emperor Dasharatha, but Valmiki also calls him *mahaan*. Often, greatness can be implied by either or both the number of kings under an emperor and how well a king manages his kingdom and is able to make it great.

So that there is no confusion, Valmiki emphasises Dasharatha's greatness in both. To do that, he constantly compares Dasharatha to both Indra, king of Gods (as an equal), and to Manu, the king amongst humans (as a protector of the human race). The following *shloka* in the 6th sarga is an example of that:

yatha manuH mahaateja lokasya parirakshitaa |
tatha raja dasharathaH lokasya parirakshitaa || 1-6-4

This *shloka* translates to, 'Like Manu, the foremost protector of mankind, King Dasharatha (while dwelling in the city of Ayodhya) protected the world.

The corresponding *shloka* in Devanagari is clubbed with other *sholkas* and mentioned below.

While, in order to rhyme the words, Valmiki uses the words raja and maharaja synonymously for King Dasharatha, the constant comparison to Indra and Manu makes it obvious that Valmiki implies that Dasharatha was more than a mere king. The *shlokas* describing the skills and abilities of Emperor Dasharatha are given below.

तस्याम् पुर्याम् अयोध्यायाम् वेदवित् सर्व संग्रहः |
दीर्घदर्शी महातेजाः पौर जानपद प्रियः || १-६-१
इक्ष्वाकूणम् अतिरथो यज्वा धर्मपरो वशी |
महर्षिकल्पो राजर्षिः त्रिषु लोकेषु विश्रुतः || १-६-२
बलवान् निहत अमित्रो मित्रवान् विजित इन्द्रियः |
धनैः च संचयैः च अन्यैः शक्र वैश्रवण उपमः || १-६-३
यथा मनुर् महातेजा लोकस्य परिरक्षिता |
तथा दशरथो राजा लोकस्य परिरक्षिता || १-६-४

tasyaam puryaam ayodhyayaam veda vit sarva
sangrahaH |
diirgha darshii mahatejaa paura janapada priyaH || 1-6-1
ikshwakuuNaam ati rathaH yaGYva dharma paraH vashii |
maharSi kalpaH rajarSi triSu lokeshu visrutaH || 1-6-2
balavaan nihata a mitraH mitravaan vijita indriyaH |
dhanaiH cha anyaiH sanchayaiH cha shakraH
vaisravanaH upamaH || 1-6-3
yatha manuH mahaateja lokasya parirakshitaa |
tatha raja dasharathaH lokasya parirakshitaa || 1-6-4

The complete English translation of the *shlokas* is: 'He who is well-versed in the Vedas, who is a gatherer of all scholars, riches and forces as well, a foreseer and a great resplendent one, also one who is esteemed by urbanites and countrymen alike, one who is a top-speeded chariot-warrior among the emperors of Ikshvaku kings, one who has performed many Vedic rituals, a virtuous one, a great controller, a saint-like kingly sage, one who he is renowned in all the three worlds, a mighty one with all his enemies eradicated, nevertheless who has friends, one who conquered all his senses, one who is similar to Indra, or Kubera on earth with his wealth, accumulations and other possessions, he that Emperor Dasharatha while dwelling in the city of Ayodhya protected the world, like Manu, the foremost protector of mankind.'

Now that we have understood Dasharatha's greatness as an emperor and the provincial kings under him, in the next section we will discuss the spread of his empire by examining the vastness of Kosala's dominion. Can you imagine how far and wide Kosala's dominion was?

The Vastness of Kosala's Dominion

In the Valmiki Ramayana, after mentioning that Maharaja Dasharatha is an emperor and has thousands of kings under his dominion, Valmiki alludes to the infinite vastness of Maharaja Dasharatha's empire in a dialogue between him and Empress Kaikeyi after she has entered *kopa bhavana* (the house of wrath). She enters the *kopa bhavana*, as she is displeased by the news of Shri Rama's coronation and wants her son to be crowned instead.

The infinite vastness of Emperor Dasharatha's empire can be compared to the never-ending rotations of a wheel. This is mentioned in the *Ayodhya Kanda*, the *kanda* after *Bala Kanda*, where Dasharatha himself speaks about it.

Emperor Dasharatha tells Kaikeyi, 'My jurisdiction over this earth stretches till the extent to which a chariot wheel revolves. Eastern (countries), Sindhu, Sauviira and Saurashtra as well as (countries on) the southward paths, Vanga, Anga, Magadha and Matsya (countries), full of riches Kasi and Kausala (countries).' The *shloka* for the corresponding dialogue is mentioned below.

यावदावर्त ते चक्रं तावती मे वसुन्धरा || २-१०-३६
प्राचीनाः सिन्धुसौवीराः सौराष्ट्रा दक्षिणापथाः |
वङ्गाङ्गमगधा मत्स्याः समृद्धाः काशिकोसलाः || २-१०-३७

yaavat aavartate chakram taavati me vasundharaa
|| 2-10-36
prachiinaaH sindhu sauviiraaH sauraashhtraaH
dakshhiNaapathaaH |
vaN^gaaN^ga magadhaaH matsyaaH kaashi
kausalaaH samR^iddhaaH || 2-10-37

Before proceeding further, it is important to point out that this *shloka* is mentioned differently on specific online versions of the Ramayana. This is with regards to the mention of *prachiinaaH*, which implies 'ancient' or 'eastern countries'. The Valmiki Ramayana of the Gita Press has the word *draviDaaH* instead of *prachiinaaH*. *DraviDaaH* in Sanskrit implies 'southern countries' and *sindhu sauviiraaH sauraashhtraaH* countries mentioned in the *shloka* are all western ones. The correct *shloka* would read: *draviDaaH sindhu sauviiraaH sauraashhtraaH dakshhiNaapathaaH.*

यावदावर्त ते चक्रं तावति मे वसुन्धरा ॥ २।१०।३६
द्रविडाः सिन्धुसौवीराः सौराष्ट्राः दक्षिणापथाः ।
वङ्गाङ्गमगधाः मत्स्याः समृद्धाः काशि कौसलाः ॥ २।१०।३७

Its correct English translation would be, 'My jurisdiction over this earth stretches till the extent to which a chariot-wheel revolves. Southern (countries), Sindhu, Sauviira and Saurastra, as well as (countries on) the southward paths, Vanga, Anga, Magadha and Matsya (countries), full of riches, Kasi and Kausala (countries).'

Emperor Dasharatha's dominion over the infinite expanse of areas, including southern countries and those countries on the southward path from Ayodhya, is reiterated in the *Sundara Kanda* when Shri Rama's ardent devotee, Hanumana, is on his way to Lanka in search of Devi Sita. While leaping across the ocean, he comes across Goddess Surasa, the mother of the Nagas. Goddess Surasa, who resides in the ocean and the netherworlds, desires to devour the leaping Hanumana. As she spots Hanumana, she opens her mouth wide enough to engulf the mighty Hanumana. On hearing about her desire, Hanumana tells Goddess Surasa that he is an emissiary of Shri Rama and is going to Lanka to look for Devi Sita. He adds, 'You live in the territory (country) of Shri Rama, so you should help him too.' Hanumana then offers to be eaten by her once his work is finished.

In this *shloka*, the territory he refers to is the ocean, which also comes on the southward path if a chariot wheel revolves from Ayodhya. In the Ramayana, Indra steals Maharaja Sagara's Ashvamedha horse. Maharaja Sagara is one of Shri Rama's forefathers. He entrusts the search of this horse to his 60,000 sons who dig up the ocean to look for it. This caused the ocean to deepen and expand. Subsequently, the ocean has been acknowledged as Saagara. The word Saagara in Sanskrit means 'son of Sagara or that which belongs to Sagara'. Since Shri Rama is a descendent of Sagara, after the death of Emperor Dasharatha, the territories of the ocean come under his dominion. This is why Hanumana suggests to the gaping-mouthed Goddess Surasa to help Shri Rama instead of causing obstructions.

The *shloka* relating to the ocean's expansion done during Maharaja Sagara's reign is in *Bala Kanda, sarga* 5. In the following *shloka*, Sage Valmiki says, 'Among them (the illustrious rulers of Ayodhya), a king named Sagara got the ocean dug (deepened and expanded) and his 60,000 sons surrounded him whenever he went (to battle).'

येषाम् स सगरो नाम सागरो येन खानितः |
षष्टिः पुत्र सहस्राणि यम् यान्तम् पर्यवारयन् ||१-५-२

yeShAm sa sagaro nAma sAgaro yena khAnitaH: |
ShaShTiH putra sahasrANi yam yAntam
paryavArayan ||1-5-2

The shloka corresponding to Hanumana reminding Goddess Surasa about her residing in the kingdom of Lord Rama is given in the *Sundara Kanda, sarga* 1.

In this *shloka*, the great devotee Hanumana says, 'I am going as Rama's emissary to search for his wife. It is proper for you to render help since you are a resident of his kingdom.'

तस्याः सकाशं दूतोऽहं गमिष्ये रामशासनात्।
कर्तुमर्हसि रामस्य साहं विषयवासिनि।।५-१-१५५

*tasyAH sakAshaM dUto.ahaM gamiShye
rAmashAsanAt |
kartumarhasi rAmasya sAhyaM
viShayavAsini | |5-1-155*

Also, it would be factually inaccurate to mention *prachiinaaH* under the dominion of Dasharatha. This is because his jurisdiction did not extend to the east and north of Kosala wherein lies the country of Videha, also known as Mithila. This is why no country in the north is mentioned under his dominion and instead, southern and western countries are.

In the Valmiki Ramayana, Devi Sita is the princess of Videha. Dasharatha is so pleased to have his two sons, Rama and Lakshmana, marry Sita and her sister Urmila that he requests Janaka's permission to allow his other two sons, Bharata and Shatrughna, to marry Sita's two paternal cousins. In this manner, he not only forges an alliance with Videha but also cements it through the marriage of all his sons with all the princesses, leaving no scope for another prince or king to enter their lives in future.

Janaka and his brother Kushadhwaja together ruled the north and east countries bordering Kosala Empire.

Their empire encompassed the territories of the present-day Nepal in the north, Bihar, Jharkhand and also parts of the east (now Bangladesh) and West Bengal. According to certain references, their influence also extended over Myanmar, which is referred to as *kiriTa desha*. There is also a brief mention of the *KiriTa* people in the palace of Shri Rama and Devi Sita, the *shloka* for this is discussed in Part IV of this book. Under any case, the kingdoms of the in-laws of Dasharatha's sons cannot be under his dominion, as they have become friendly countries after the marriages. Therefore, it is inaccurate to mention the eastern countries under his jurisdiction.

It is intriguing to note that Emperor Dasharatha says that his jurisdiction is as infinite as the revolutions of the chariot wheel. This gives us an idea of a never-ending empire, just the way the Romans, thousands of years later, viewed theirs as *imperium sine fine*—an 'empire without end'.

Now that the vastness of Kosala, the extent of its dominion and the location of its power centre Ayodhya have been deciphered, let's discover the size and shape of Ayodhya in Part III of this book. Can you guess what the shape of Ayodhya was and how big it was?

Part III

SHAPES, PLANS AND LAYOUTS: THE EXTERIOR DESIGN OF AYODHYA

In this part of the book, we will discuss what the district of Ayodhya looked like, its shape and how it was designed to secure itself against invasions. Details of Ayodhya's size and the exterior design of Ayodhya will also be examined.

What Was the Shape of Ayodhya?

Ayodhya had an interesting layout. In today's maps, most cities look like splotched eggs on a pan. But not Ayodhya. Below is an example of a splotched-egg city of New Delhi sourced from Google Maps 2019. The map of Delhi is shared as a comparison because both Ayodhya and New Delhi are capitals of countries. Ayodhya was the capital of the former empire of Kosala (Bharat), while New Delhi is the capital of today's Bharat.

Compared with any existing city or district of India today, Ayodhya was different in numerous ways. Ayodhya followed the ancient Hindu science of architecture called *Vastu Shastra*, therefore, it was rectangular in shape. According to *Vastu Shastra*, the best shapes for settlements are rectangular, square, bow or lotus-like. All these shapes follow particular ratios for settlement creation. Random ratios are not taken for choosing the length and breath of the town or city. Even villages have dedicated shapes and ratios to choose from. Town planning was rather exemplary in ancient Bharat.

Almost all cities of ancient India were based on the principles of *Vastu Shastra*. On the adjacent page is an example of another rectangular city of ancient Bharat, which subscribed to the norms of *Vastu Shastra*. The ruins of this rectangular city, now named Dholavira, were found in the state of Gujarat. Dholavira is located in Khadir Bet, Bhachau taluka in Gujarat's Kutch district. In the local language, *bet* means island. The island is surrounded by the vast emptiness of the Great Rann of Kutch. The image has been sourced from *Archeological Survey of India*.

In the next chapter, the size of Ayodhya will be discussed. In the Valmiki Ramayana, the size of Ayodhya is given in the ancient Hindu system of measurement called *yojana*. Can you guess the dimensions of Ayodhya in *yojana*?

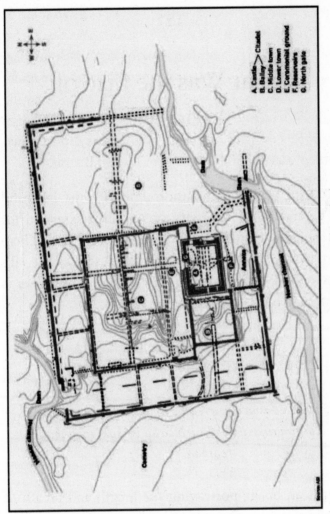

The Layout of Dholavira

What Was the Size of Ayodhya?

With well laid out thoroughfares, the beautiful and prosperous city of Ayodhya extended for 12 *yojanas* in length and for 3 *yojanas* in breadth. These are the words with which Valmiki describes the size of Ayodhya, in *sarga* 5 of *Bala Kanda*. The *shloka* is mentioned below.

आयता दश च द्वे च योजनानि महापुरी |
श्रीमती त्रीणि विस्तीर्णा सु विभक्ता महापथा || १-५-७

aayataa dasha cha dve cha yojanaani mahaa purii |
shriimatii triiNi vistiirNaa su vibhaktaa mahaa
pathaa | | 1-5-7

Next is an image portraying the length and breath of Ayodhya as 12 *yojanas* long and 3 *yojanas* wide. The image, though proportionate to 12:3 ratio, is not to scale. The image points northwards.

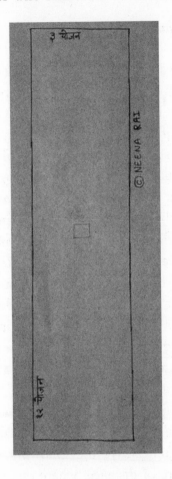

Since the shape and dimensions of Ayodhya are now established, a better understanding of *yojana* is required to decipher the size of Ayodhya in comparison to the current sizes of our cities and districts. Without deciphering how long a *yojana* is, one cannot get a clear picture of the area of Ayodhya. This will be done in the following section.

What Is a *Yojana*?

The Hindu system of measurements is different from the Western system. Large lengths are measured in *yojanas* in the Hindu system. In the Western system, large lengths of distance are measured in miles. In India today, large distances are measured in kilometres where one mile is equal to approximately 1.609 kilometre.

All Sanskrit dictionaries define *yojana* as a Vedic measurement of distance used in ancient Bharat. According to the *Vedic Index of Names and Subjects*, the word *yojana* occurs frequently in the *Rig Veda*. There is no reference defining its real length, but it is reckoned at 4 *kroshas*, or about 9 miles or 14.5 kilometres. Many books give us the definitions and commentaries of *yojana*. For the purpose of this book, a list of various commentators and translators referred to are mentioned in the Bibliography.

Shri Desiraju Hanumanta Rao, who translated the Ramayana to English, in his commentary in valmikiramayan.net says the following: '*Yojana* is an ancient measure of distance, where one *yojana* roughly equals 8 to 10 miles. Its account is like this : 1 *angula* = 3/4 inch; 4 *angulas* = one *dhanu graha* (bow grip); 8 *angulas* = one *dhanu muSTi* (fist with thumb raised); 12 *angulas* = 1 *vitasti* (distance between tip of thumb and tip of last finger when palm is stretched); 2 *vitastis* = 1 *aratni* (cubit); 4 *aratnis* = one *danDa, dhanuS* (bow height of 6 feet); 10 *danDa*-s = 1 *rajju* (60 feet); 2 *rajjus* = 1 *paridesha* (120 feet); 2, 000 *dhanuSs* = one *krosha, goraTa* (4,000 yards); 4 *kroshas* = 1 *yojana*. Thus, 1 yojana is 9–10 miles. But the British revenue measurement system scaled it down to five miles, and all the dictionaries say that one *yojana* is five miles. But traditionally, it is held as 10 miles. More information on these measures can be found in the *Arthashastra* by Kautilya.'

On the other hand, A.C. Bhaktivedanta Swami Prabhupada gives the equivalent length of a *yojana* to be about 13 kilometres (8 miles) throughout his translations of the *Bhagavata Purana*. Prabhupada was a famous Hindu spiritual teacher and the founder of the International Society for Krishna Consciousness (ISKCON).

The information obtained from the dictionaries and commentators are not contradictory, but they have slight differences. If one can do basic mathematics, one can calculate the length of a *yojana* oneself. Consider the following measurements.

1 *danda/dhanush* = 6 feet
2,000 *danda/dhanush* = 1 *krosha*
4 *krosha* = 1 *yojana*

Therefore, 6 x 2,000 = 12,000 feet = 1 *krosha*
4 x 12,000 feet = 48,000 feet = 1 *yojana*

A mile has exactly 5,280 feet in it. Therefore, in order to calculate the number of miles in a yojana we divide 48,000 by 5,280 and we get 9.09090909. Therefore, nine miles (approx.) equals one *yojana*.

Using this calculation, we can calculate the area of Ayodhya in square miles. To read the results in square kilometres, for an approximate result, multiply the length value (1 mile) by 1.609.

In miles

Length: 12 x 9 miles = 108 miles

Width: 3 x 9 miles = 27 miles

Total covered area of Ayodhya = 108 x 27 = 2,916 square miles or 4,692 square kilometres approximately.

So what could be the smaller size of Ayodhya (based on A.C. Bhaktivedanta Swami Prabhupada's definition)?

In miles

Length: 12 x 8 miles = 96 miles

Width: 3 x 8 miles = 24 miles

Total covered area of Ayodhya = 96 x 24 = 2,304 square miles or 3,707 square kilometres approximately.

But why does Prabhupada's definition have a smaller conversion for *yojana*?

The difference in miles is probably because of the size of a *danda* or a staff. The *dhanush* (bow) is known to be the same size or height as the *danda*, therefore, in many places these two values are interchangeable. The length of both the *danda* or *dhanush* is equal to the average height of man.

The change in A.C. Bhaktivedanta Swami Prabhupada's calculation is most probably based on the lower height used for the *danda*. It is very likely he has used the height of the *danda* as 5 feet and 5 inches, which is the average height of citizens of Bharat today. In ancient Bharat, however, according to the Hindu *shastras*, the average height of the Hindus (in previous yugas) was more than 6 feet. Some Hindu historians have mentioned that people born to affluent families were as tall as 7 feet like those from the princely families who are mentioned in *itihasa*.

Being so tall is not surprising, as a person's height is based on a set of genetic and nutritional factors. The average height of citizens of Bharat is lower today because of bad nutrition (due to poverty and other factors like adulteration of food, specifically milk). At present, there are many tall populations in the world who are perhaps the same height as those mentioned in the Hindu *shastras*.

Let's take, for example, the Dutch. They are the tallest people in the world, with the average height being 1.838 metres or 6.03 feet. According to the military data of the Netherlands, the average height of their men increased 20 centimetres in only the last 150 years. That is almost an increase of eight inches over a short span of 150 years. The World Health Organization determines that quality of life and a good diet consisting of dairy products and cold-water fish may have contributed to the Dutch population's tall stature.

Similar to the one consumed by the Dutch, a diet that includes milk products, grains, vegetables, fruits and fish is mentioned in various places in the Ramayana. Deer and boar meat were consumed in the jungles. The consumption of these products varied across races and classes of people. Another interesting fact to note is that all government buildings in the Netherlands have tall doorways. This was evident in Ayodhya too. Therefore, the average height for Hindus in the Treta Yuga and also the *danda* is taken to be 6 feet. The same height is used for calculation of distances.

Now let's consider the topic of 'area'. Ayodhya, the district whose 'area' covers 2,916 square miles or 4,692 square kilometres, seems rather large even today. Very few cities in the world are this big today. In the current era, the city/metro area that is about the same size as Ayodhya is Philadelphia at 4,661 square kilometres. The data for Philadelphia's area is based on an article called 'The Largest Cities in the World' in worldatlas. com in 2019. Shared below is the data on the largest cities of the world by land area.

Largest Cities in the World By Land Area

Rank	Metro Area	Area (Km sq)
1	New York	8,683
2	Tokyo	6,993
3	Chicago	5,498
4	Atlanta	5,083
5	Philadelphia	4,661
6	Boston	4,497
7	Los Angeles	4,320
8	Dallas	3,644
9	Houston	3,355

In comparison, New Delhi covers an area of 573 square miles or 1,484 square kilometres and is the largest city in terms of area in India. It is worth mentioning here that another Hindu epic composed by Veda Vyasa, Mahabharata, refers to Delhi or Indraprastha as a 'village' that was supposed to be handed over to the *Pandavas*.

13

How Populated Was Ayodhya?

Western cities or districts today have much lower populations compared to their Asian counterparts. This was the case in the previous yugas too.

The Valmiki Ramayana states that Ayodhya was densely populated. In terms of population, little has changed from ancient Bharat to current India. According to worldatlas.com, Mumbai is the second most densely populated city in the world (based on per square metre comparison). Dhaka, Chennai, Kolkata and Kathmandu all make it comfortably to the top 10 list.

Valmiki remarks in *sarga* 5 of *Bala Kanda* that there were so many people in the capital of Ayodhya that there was no space to be seen anywhere (because of too many homes). Here, a distinction has to be made between Ayodhya *purii* and Ayodhya *nagarii*. It is the capital city that is populated because in the district of Ayodhya, there are farms as well.

गृह गाढाम् अविच्छिद्राम् सम भूमौ निवेशिताम् |
शालि तण्डुल संपूर्णाम् इक्षु काण्ड रसः उदकाम् ||१-५-१७

gR^iha gaaDhaam a vi cChidraam sama bhuumau niveshitaam |
shaali taNDula sampuurNaam ikshu kaNDa rasa udakaam || 1-5-17

The exact translation of the *shloka* above is, 'The housing is very dense and there is no place or ground unutilised, and all are constructed on well-levelled lands, and *shaali* rice grain is plentiful, while the drinking water tastes like sugarcane juice.' Most commentators like that of Gita Press have interpreted this as 'heavily populated with houses occupying every inch of the urban capital of Ayodhya'.

Sadly, there is no exact number of people mentioned in the Ramayana. It is very likely that the kingdom of Kosala, too, maintained a census just like today. We can deduce this because ancient Ayodhya did keep a track of the exact number of animals, chariots and soldiers in their armies. This is discussed in Part VI of the book. For now, let's figure out how Ayodhya was designed to protect itself from enemies.

14

How Was Ayodhya Designed to Protect It from Enemies?

In ancient times, every district, regardless of whether it contained the capital within it or not, had various types of defences. While most defence is solely assumed as the presence of the military and weapons, in earlier times, defence was very smartly encapsulated in the design of the habitation itself.

A few key features of such inbuilt designer defence systems included moats, forests, dry lands, hills, stones and high walls of the fortress. The high wall of the fortress and the rampart were further designed in such a way that cannons and other defence equipment could be placed easily on them. Soldiers could shoot arrows through the measured gaps constructed on the walls of the ramparts. High watchtowers for the soldiers were constructed so that the enemy could be spotted from a distance.

Two key points that we will discuss in this part are the moat of Ayodhya and the forest, referred to as the 'Girdle of Trees'. The specialised weapons encapsulated in the defence of the fortress will be discussed in Part V of this book.

The Moat of Ayodhya

A moat is a large, often very deep and broad ditch that is dug around a castle, fort, fortress, building or even a town. It may or may not be filled with water. In ancient times, a moat was encapsulated in the design to serve as a fundamental and primary line of defence against a marauding army.

The moat around a castle, town or fortress worked as an obstacle outside the walls of that establishment. Moats could be natural for forts or fortresses if they were built on islands or they could be man-made too. In ancient Bharat, different types of moats could be constructed. The *Arthashastra* written by Kautilya gives exact specifications for the construction of a moat where the use of burnt bricks and detailed feet by feet planning is prescribed.

The next image is that of Angkor Wat, Cambodia. It has a rather large and beautiful moat encircling it. The greenery around the moat is quite prominent as well. Angkor Wat is a temple complex in Cambodia and is the largest religious monument in the world. The temple was originally constructed as a Hindu temple dedicated to Lord Vishnu for the Khmer Empire by King Suryavarman II in the early 12th century in Yasodharapura. This bewitching temple complex adheres to the principles of *Vastu* to the T. Notice the rectangular shape of the temple complex as well, which is similar to both Dholavira and Ayodhya.

In Valmiki Ramayana, there is a clear reference to Ayodhya having a moat. Almost all castles and forts in the Ramayanic Era had moats. According to the Ramayana, even Lanka had a moat. Nagesh Bhatta, in his commentary on Valmiki Ramayana says, 'Ayodhya had deep moats filled with water surrounding it, which prevented the entry of friends and foes alike.'

'That Ayodhya is an impassable one for trespassers, or for others invaders, owing to her impassable and profound moats,' is mentioned in the translation by Desiraju Hanumanta Rao. The corresponding *shloka* with reference to the moat from the Valmiki Ramayana is given below. The *shloka* is from *sarga* 5 of *Bala Kanda*.

दुर्ग गंभीर परिखाम् दुर्गाम् अन्यैः दुरासदम् |
वाजीवारण संपूर्णाम् गोभिः उष्ट्रैः खरैः तथा || १-५-१३

durga gambhiira parikhaam durgaam anyaiH
duraasadam |
vaajii vaarana sampuurNam gobhiH uSTraiH
kharaiH tatha | | 1-5-13

According to this *shloka*, the fortress was difficult to get to because of the presence of the moat, which was difficult to cross because of its width and depth. To give an idea of how deep the moat was, the Sanskrit word *parikhaam* is used. It implies a moat or a ditch deep enough for an elephant to easily drown.

It is fascinating to note that the word 'moat' is mentioned in plural for the one in Ayodhya by most commentators and translators. While it was common practice to have a singular moat, multiple moats were not very prevalent. Often, moats with three sections (multiples) were also referred to as a moat. It is not clear whether Ayodhya had a single or multiple moats, but one can always turn to prudent Kautilya to understand the presence and construction of multiple moats.

In the *Arthashastra* by Kautilya, specific dimensions of moats are mentioned. These are related to the height of the fort wall. He says, 'Three moats are to be built at regular intervals.' These details can be found in chapters relating to the 'Construction of Forts'.

After the instructions about the number of moats, Kautilya provides exact dimensions for the construction of each of them. He specifically states, 'Round this fort, three ditches with an intermediate space of 1 *danda* (6 feet) from each other, 14, 12 and 10 *dandas* respectively in width, with depth less by one-quarter or by one-half of their width, square at their bottom and one-third as wide as at their top, with sides built of stones or bricks, filled with perennial flowing water or with water drawn from some other source.'

Considering the massive size of Ayodhya, an assumption can be made that the moat may have been larger than the size Kautilya mentions. However, if one goes with his directions, the three-phased or partitioned moat is between 70 and 100 metres wide. It is possible that just like Kautilya's states, the waters of river Sarayu were harnessed to feed the moats surrounding Ayodhya.

It is imperative to mention here that while multiple moats may have been uncommon, they were not present just during the ancient times. Strongholds with multiple moats were constructed even till a few hundred years ago. Below are some images of multiple moats as a means to safeguard a stronghold. The first image is from Fort Bourtange (Dutch: *Vesting Bourtange*) from the village of Bourtange, Groningen, Netherlands. The image has been uploaded by user Bourtange on Wikipedia. This medieval fort was built under William the Silent and completed in 1593. Notice that this fort has three different moats or one moat with three partitions. Each portion is separated by an evenly measured land mass. This moat is not only enchanting to look at, but surprisingly follows the three-phased design Kautilya speaks about. The fort is in the shape of a pentagon, therefore the corresponding moat also follows the same shape.

Interestingly enough, this fort, like Ayodhya, is a town where people still reside. Below is the proper layout, the atlas version of the fortified town of Bourtange. This image has been sourced from Atlas van Loon, Wikipedia.

While one may argue or agree that there could have been one or three moats protecting the fortress of Ayodhya, Kautilya has given a very clear description about what the moat needs to contain. In the *Arthashastra*, in the chapter dedicated to the construction of forts he specifies: 'Filled with perennial flowing water or with water drawn from some other source, and possessing crocodiles and lotus plants shall the moat be constructed.'

It is indeed gripping to imagine a moat full of crocodiles and other aquatic animals. The presence of lotus would not only make it look beautiful but would also provide hiding places for fish. And fish are food for crocodiles, especially when enemies are not becoming crocodile feed.

Such moats with lotuses can be seen in countries in the east even today. Below are two beautiful images of moats with lotuses from China and Japan. The first image of the moat filled with lotuses is from the Imperial City in Beijing clicked by user Francisco Anzola, Wikipedia. Like Ayodhya, the Imperial City, too, was surrounded by a wall and a moat.

Next is an image captured by そらみみ, on Wikipedia, of the north moat of Fukuoka Castle in Japan. The castle is situated on top of Fukusaki hill. In this beautiful picture, the lotus buds are about to bloom.

Now that we have covered the moat as a form of defence around Ayodhya, let's discuss the Girdle of Trees around Ayodhya in the next section of this chapter.

The Girdle of Trees

While just having a moat sufficed as defence for most forts or fortresses, this was not the case for Ayodhya. The moat around Ayodhya's stronghold, according to Valmiki, was neither the only form nor the primary form of defence against invading armies. For Ayodhya, the moat was the secondary line of defence because the preliminary one was outside the moat—in the form of a dense jungle. The dense jungle was full of Sal trees and encircled Ayodhya like a girdle.

Most commentators of the Valmiki Ramayana are not very clear about the exact placement of the trees, even though in earlier times, trees and forests were found to be encircling certain fortresses. The presence of thick forest was considered as a deterrent for invading armies. This sort of a forest encircling a stronghold need not be confused with a stronghold constructed in the jungle itself.

Specific forts and fortresses constructed in the jungles were known as *Vana Durga* in Sanskrit. These *Vana Durgas* protected the forest lands of the kingdoms and the population was not housed there. They are often loosely translated to hunting palaces in English. All kingdoms in the past used to own forests where animal breeding was ensured. Hunting and war game simulations were conducted in these forests to keep their king and kinsmen in top shape. These *Vana Durgas* can be compared to the various military encampments in far-off places where war games and military exercises are conducted by the modern armies of the world. These war games, like in the olden times, are conducted to test the combat readiness of the participating armies. They also serve as a show of strength and tactics between the competing military men or armed forces. Therefore, while the fortress of Ayodhya was surrounded by a dense jungle, it should not be confused as a *Vana Durga*.

The jungle of Ayodhya is clearly described by Valmiki in two *shlokas* from *sarga 5*, *Bala Kanda*. Sage Valmiki in the second line of the shloka says, 'Beyond the uncrossable moats of Ayodhya, the fortress was encircled by a girdle of trees.' This is the first *shloka* that describes the jungle of Ayodhya.

वधू नाटक सन्चैः च संयुक्ताम् सर्वतः पुरीम् |
उद्यान आम्र वणोपेताम् महतीम् साल मेखलाम् || १-५-१२

vadhuu naaTaka sanghaiH cha samyuktaam sarvataH
puriim |
udyaana aamra vana upetaam mahatiim saala
mekhalaam || 1-5-12

The phrase Valmiki uses in this *shloka* is *mahatiim saala mekhalaam. Saala* is the Sanskrit word for the Sal tree. The word *mekhalaam* in Sanskrit means a girdle.

Wearing a girdle in Hindu culture is rather common. A girdle is called a *kardhani* or a *kamar bandh. Kardhani* is a Hindi word for a waistband or a girdle and is often used interchangeably with a *kamar bandh.* While a *kamar bandh* could be made up of fabric, a *kardhani* is ideally made up of precious metals, shells and even ivory.

Such an ornamental girdle is worn as a belt or as a cord around the waist. The typical choice of metal for an ornamental girdle or *kardhani* is gold or silver. Often, it has bells too and is worn above a sari or a dhoti.

Shared next are two images of women wearing the *kardhani.* The first is of a Cambodian dancer taken by Beth Kanter, Wikipedia. Here the pretty dancer is wearing a *sampot,* which is like the Indian *dhoti* or sari. There are many types of *sampots,* but most are tied at the waist and held up using a golden belt. This golden belt is called the *kardhani* in Hindi and a *mekhalaa* in Sanskrit.

The second image is of the Indian Odissi classical dancer Sitara Thobani. It has been uploaded by Brendan from Vancouver on Wikipedia. In this image, the gorgeous dancer sports an elaborately detailed *kardhani*, which has three separate lines of decorative patterns.

The *kardhani* is a multipurpose ornament that not only helps women to keep their *sari* or *dhoti* or *sampot* held together on the waist but also serves as a decorative ornament. Therefore, since ancient times, the *kardhani* has played an important role as a part of the ensemble of Hindu women. For many women, the safety pin invented in October 1849, replaced the utility of the *kardhani* to hold nine yards of fabric together.

With these two examples it is quite clear that Valmiki
refers to the jungle surrounding Ayodhya as a *mekhalaa*,
which upholds, protects and surrounds the moat of
Ayodhya. When describing Ayodhya as well as Lanka
in the Ramayana, Valmiki refers to both these cities
in the feminine and describes them as a lady with her
clothes and ornaments. The moat of Lanka is referred
to as the dress of the lady and the jungle of Ayodhya as
the ornamental girdle.

Going further, a *shloka* from *sarga* 6 of *Bala Kanda*
throws light on the area of the jungle and confirms
the size of the extended boundary of Ayodhya beyond
the ramparts. The translation of this *shloka* is, 'While
residing in that city (from where) King Dasharatha
ruled the world, that city is further fortified up to two
more *yojanas* outside the city, true to its name Ayodhya,
an unassailable one.'

सा योजने च द्वे भूयः सत्यनामा प्रकाशते |
यस्याम् दशरथो राजा वसन् जगत् अपालयत् || १-६-२६

saa yojane cha dve bhuuyaH satya naama prakaashate |
yasyaam raajaa dasharathaH vasan jagat apaalayat |￼| 1-6-26

This *shloka* implies that beyond the four walls of the city
of Ayodhya and its moat, a girdle of Sal trees extended
upto two more *yojanas*. Perhaps, apart from the Sal trees,
other means of making the terrain dangerous, as part of
fortification of the jungle, may have been employed by
King Dasharatha. But Valmiki does not clarify the same;
instead, he just mentions that fortifications in the form
of a Sal tree jungle, upto two *yojanas* wide, surrounded

Ayodhya and its moat. He further implies that owing to all of this—the girdle of Sal trees, and the previously mentioned fortifications, the moat, the rampart, the *shataghnii* (a type of weapon explained in Part V)—Ayodhya is unassailable. It is to be reminded that the word Ayodhya itself means 'that which is unassailable' or 'that which cannot be fought or conquered'.

A question arises here with regard to the specific mention of Sal trees. Why was this particular tree grown around Ayodhya? What is special about Sal trees?

What Is Special about Sal Trees?

Sage Valmiki does not mention the Sal tree casually. There is a reason behind him naming every variety of vegetation in the *Ramayana*. The Sal tree's botanical name is *Shorea robusta*. In Hindu tradition, the Sal tree is said to be favoured by Lord Vishnu. In Kali Yuga, Sal is also revered by Buddhists because it is said that Queen Maya gave birth to Gautam Buddha under this tree. According to certain Hindu sages, Buddha is considered to be the ninth avatar of Lord Vishnu.

This tree is native to the Indian subcontinent. While it may be commonly found, this tree is no less than an amazing gift to India. Every part of this tree is useful in some way—from making homes with its wood to feeding its leaves to cattle, from using its resin for Ayurvedic formulations to caulking boats. The wood of the Sal tree, unlike other varieties of wood, does not rot easily in water. There are many reasons why the Sal tree is mentioned by Sage Valmiki and it was most likely cultivated on purpose by the state of Ayodhya.

Below is an image of a Sal tree forest in Nepal captured by Krish Dulal, Wikipedia. Along with it is an image of the Sal leaf captured by Mr Garg, also found on Wikipedia. Both images are used for illustrative purposes.

Even today, dry leaves of Sal are stitched together to make eco-friendly plates and bowls. They are called *patravali* or *pattal*. The used leaves and plates of *pattal* are then fed to goats and cows.

Sal finds itself readily used as an astringent, anti-inflammatory and antibacterial ingredient in Ayurvedic medicines. Its resin, known as Sal *dammar* or Indian *dammar*, is often burned as incense in Hindu ceremonies. Since ancient times, the resin has also been used as a varnish and to caulk boats and ships.

Oil extracted from the Sal seed is used for cooking. It is also used for lamp oil. The fruit of this tree, which flowers in March–April, often finds itself turned into vegetable fat. It is no wonder that the citizens of Ayodhya had the city encircled by a jungle of such an amazing tree.

Now that we have understood the exterior structure and design of Ayodhya, in the next part we will understand the interiors and the designer details of Ayodhya.

Part IV

DESIGNER DETAILS: DESCRIBING THE INSIDES OF AYODHYA

The interiors of Ayodhya can be described in many words, but the one that comes to mind first is spectacular. When discussing the design of ancient-era precincts, the inside of any district is a description of what is contained within the high-walled boundaries of its stronghold. This includes the roadways, the highways, the castle, the watchtowers, the palaces, the living quarters, the farms and the gardens. Sage Valmiki gives us a lot of information to decode the inner design of Ayodhya.

In Part II of this book, we have ascertained that:

- Ayodhya was a large district (Ayodhya *Nagarii*), which contained a city of the same name.
- In the district of Ayodhya, there were urban and rural areas.
- Urban areas of Ayodhya *Nagarii* consisted of the capital district as well as the diplomatic area (*pur*).
- Ayodhya's diplomatic centre/capital district was where the emperor resided with his important ministers (Ayodhya *Purii*).

With the aim of describing Ayodhya accurately, one has to depend on a dispersed set of information across multiple sources. One of the most important facts obtained about Ayodhya through commentators is that its internal design, like its external boundaries, was made according to *Vastu Shastra*.

The *Vastu Shastra* text on which the city layout was planned is called *Manasara Vastu Shastra*. This *shastra*, written by Sage Manasara, is a definitive Hindu treatise on *Vastu*. It elaborately deals with town planning in ancient Bharat. Sage Manasara also wrote the *Manasara*

Shilpa Shastra, which deals with the science of art and craft and it entails various rules and principles of sculpture and Hindi iconography.

The word *shastra* means a body of work, rules, manual, book or treatise. In ancient Hindu literature, this word is used as a suffix. It denotes technical or very specialised knowledge in a defined area of practice, which could have encapsulated the work done by previous sages as well. For example, in his book *Arthashastra*, Kautilya compiles the wisdom of many sages.

According to *Manasara*, prosperous towns are located near rivers and seas, preferably on their shores. Lanka and Ayodhya were both prosperous districts: Lanka near the sea and Ayodhya near the Sarayu River. To become famous and abundant, a district or a mega city should have a river to its north that flows towards the east. This placement provides for the district's global success. Ayodhya fulfilled both these criteria. Sarayu was on the north of the district and flowed towards the east. No wonder Ayodhya has always been famous around the world.

Next is an example of the outline for towns and forts from the book *Architecture of Manasara*, sourced from the Archeological Survey of India. This is a simple outline of a *nagara*. On the top left hand side, it is mentioned that this is the layout of a *rajdhaniya* type of *nagara*, which implies 'a *nagara* with the capital'. It is believed that Ayodhya *Nagarii* had a similar design.

In the image, one can observe the royal palace situated in the centre of the *nagara*. Ideally, a *purii* has four gates, one in each direction. The capital district connects with the rest of the stronghold through highways, which leads into the centre through these gates. These four highways extend to the outer extremity of the district or the stronghold. They divide the district or its urban part in four equal quarters.

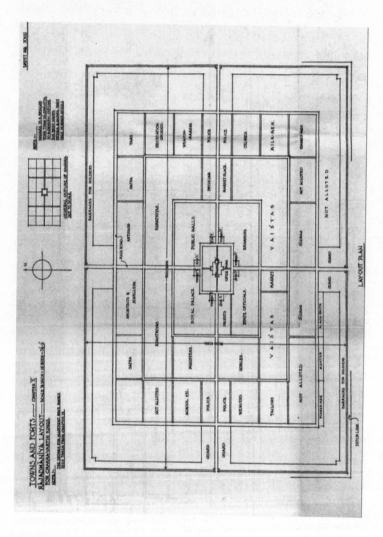

Ayodhya, too, had the same design. Since the highways and roadways are lifelines of any district, we will first start by studying these to understand Ayodhya's internal design.

15

The Roadways of Ayodhya

Various references are given to the beautiful roadways of Ayodhya in the Valmiki Ramayana. Ayodhya had large highways, which connected the district from corner to corner. These highways were constructed to allow incoming and outgoing traffic of chariots, implying that they had two lanes. One highway dissected the district from the north to south and the other from east to west. These highways extended to the external borders of the fortress, but stopped at the capital district within the city. They did not cross the innermost areas of the city, which would often be the sanctum sanctorum or *garbha griha* of the city, and usually had a temple within it. This sort of highway design enabled the king and his men to move swiftly to the end of their stronghold in an emergency. The royal palace was always connected with these royal highways, which were also called raja *bithii* or raja *maarga* in Sanskrit.

If a person stood at the centre of Ayodhya *purii*, its *garbha griha*, here is how the highways would be seen by him. Remember, the highway did not dissect the *garbha griha*, instead the *garbha griha* acted like a rectangular pivot for the highways.

- A highway running towards the north end of the stronghold from the centre of the *purii* or capital district.

- A highway running towards the south end of the stronghold from the centre of the *purii* or capital district.
- A highway running towards the west end of the stronghold from the centre of the *purii* or capital district.
- A highway running towards the east end of the stronghold from the centre of the *purii* or capital district.

The well-laid out four central highways of Ayodhya were not like the usual roads of today—black and hot like burning coals. In the peak Indian summer, one can end up with roasted soles while walking on these roads barefoot. Because of the heat in India, these roads made up of bitumen, become unbearably hot.

Contrary to today's roads, the highways of Ayodhya were not only pleasant but a pleasure to walk barefoot on. These highways always had flowers strewn on them and were continually wetted with water.

The concept behind wetting the highways was to keep them cool, so that residents could walk barefoot without feeling uncomfortable. In addition, water must have been sprinkled to keep them dust-free by mitigating the rustling up of dust that arises in the wake of passing chariots.

Even today, one can find people in India from the smallest of shops sprinkling water in front so that their establishment and the area surrounding it does not get dusty. Since earlier times and even now in certain areas, this was carried out by professional water bearers. Called Bhishti, they would sprinkle water on the roads and also provide drinking water to people on the road, in temples, parks and markets. The following image sourced from the Bodleian Library is of one such

Bhishti painted beautifuly in the Kalighat style of art, in 1875.

The word 'bhishti' is derived from the Sanskrit *vRRiShTi*, which means rain, sprinkling or shower. Also, *vRRiShTi-kara* in Sanskrit means producing rain, sprinkling or raining. The word *kara* means 'what makes' or 'maker'.

It is common to pronounce the letter V as B or Bhi in Prakrit languages spoken along the Gangetic plains. There are many reasons attributed for this mispronounciation, the main one being that V is absent from their vocabulary and another reason being that both the letters V - व (va) and B - ब (ba) are almost identical in Sanskrit. Therefore, the Sanskrit name Vivek becomes Bibek, Vijay becomes Bijay and so on.

Another reason for pronouncing V as B or Bhi is that in *Kaithi Lipi* or Kaithi script, ब (ba) is written as व (va). This script is similar to the ancient Brahmi script, which predates the current Devanagri script. It was the most widely used script for legal and admistrative works through various north Indian states. This is the script for languages like Angika, Awadhi, Bhojpuri, Hindustani, Maithili and Nagpuri.

Since ancient times, flowers, the providers of beauty, joy, food and medicines have been considered sacred in Hindu culture because they are a gift to humanity. It is their giving nature that makes them sacred. Flowers, even when their petals are crushed, still deliver gifts by releasing beautiful scents. Therefore, various gestures include the presence of flowers as an offering or decoration, both to the gods and humans.

The practice of placing flowers or flower petals on the streets or showering on visitors is a gesture of welcome. It is considered sacred even today, especially when flowers are placed for walking during the festival season or during a celebration. Today, this practice is actively retained in romantic indulgences, but this sort of a welcome was common in Ayodhya—so common that the highways of Ayodhya were always strewn with flowers.

An example of such a request for a floral welcome (in today's era) has been romantically encapsulated in a famous Hindi song called 'Baharon Phool Barsao' from the film *Suraj* (1966). The song is pictured on Rajendra Kumar and Vyjayanthimala, where actor Rajendra Kumar sings '*Oh the season of spring, please shower flowers, my lover has arrived.*'

In Hindu tradition, brides are welcomed home by decorating the entrances of homes with a rangoli or 'floral decorations of varied colours'. These decorations are both sacred as well as traditional. The rangoli, too, is a gesture of welcome. Apart from that, the marital bed on the wedding night is also decorated with rose petals strewn on the bed as a gesture of welcome.

During Diwali, Hindu families create floral decorations and rangoli at the entrances of their homes to welcome Goddess Lakshmi. Such practices are an innate part of Hindu culture and it is considered extremely offensive to ruin a floral pattern or rangoli made on the floor. Given below is an image of a beautiful rangoli on the floor captured by user skeeze on Wikipedia.

In sync with the indigenous Hindu culture of strewing flowers and wetting the roads, Sage Valmiki describes the national highways of Ayodhya in an excellent fashion. In *sarga* 5 of *Bala Kanda*, he says, 'That city shines forth with well-laid great royal highways that are always wetted with water, and with flowers strewn and scattered on them.'

राज मार्गेण महता सुविभक्तेन शोभिता |
मुक्ता पुष्प अवकीर्णेन जल सिक्तेन नित्यशः || १-५-८

raja maargeNa mahataa su vibhaktena shobhitaa |
muktaa puSpa avakiirNena jala siktena nityashaH || 1-5-8

The Sanskrit word *su vibhaktena* means beautifully divided into proportionate parts, implying that the highways were well-laid out. Then Valmiki says: *puSpa avakiirNena*, which means that 'flowers are poured or covered upon' the royal highways. He further adds, '*Jala siktena nityashaH*, meaning that the highways are 'constantly wetted with water'.

After this *shloka*, Valmiki again refers to the royal highways of Ayodhya decorated with flowers and wetted with water, along with a lot of other arrangements to welcome the four princess brides of the four princes of Ayodhya after their wedding in Videha.

The following is a lovely *shloka*, in *sarga* 77 of *Bala Kanda*, describing their welcome.

चोदयामास ताम् सेनाम् जगाम आशु ततः पुरीम् |
पताका ध्वजिनीम् रंयाम् तूर्य उद् घुष्ट निनादिताम् || १-७७-६
सिक्त राज पथा रंयाम् प्रकीर्ण कुसुम उत्कराम् |
राज प्रवेश सुमुखैः पौरैः मंगल पाणिभिः || १-७७-७
संपूर्णम् प्राविशत् राजा जन ओघैः समलंकृताम् |

codayaamaasa taam senaam jagaama aashu tataH:
puriim |
pataakaa dhvajiniim ramyaam tuurya ud ghuSTa
ninaaditaam || 1-77-6
sikta raaja pathaa ramyaam prakiirNa kusuma
utkaraam |
raaja pravesha sumukhaiH: pauraiH: mangala
paaNibhiH: || 1-77-7
sampuurNaam praavishat raajaa jana oghaiH:
sam alamkR^itaam |

The literal translation for this *shloka* is, 'Then King
Dasharatha ordered that legion to move ahead, and
then they all went towards delightful city Ayodhya,
whose royal highways are wetted with water, sprinkled
with bunches of flowers, decorated with banners and
bannerettes up above them, and reverberating with
high-sounding bugle-horns. Further, those highways
are replete with urbanites who are holding welcoming
kits of golden handy-crates and plates in which lit
camphor, fragrant incenses, vermilion powder, flowers
to shower on the incomers are arranged, and those
highways are well-decorated with throngs of people
who are glee-faced at their king's re-entry, and into
such an exhilarating city Ayodhya King Dasharatha
and his retinue entered.'

In the explanation between this *shloka* of *sarga* 77 and the previous *shloka* of *sarga* 6, there is a slight difference. For the *shloka* of *sarga* 77, Valmiki uses the words *prakiirNa kusuma utkaraam*. The (extra) word *utkaraam* in Sanskrit means scattered upward or heaped (in multitude). Valmiki uses it on purpose to imply that in addition to the flowers (usually) laid out on the highways, in order to welcome the four princess brides, the welcoming party heaped multitudes of flowers or scattered them by throwing them upwards on the highways. Even today, according to Hindu customs, flower petals are thrown upwards in the welcome of a special person. Like an elephant takes water or mud in his snout and then throws it back at himself, this is how people from the front shower petals at guests who are behind them.

To illustrate the culture of streets filled with flowers, the following image from Thailand is shared where Buddhist monks are walking on flower petals. These petals were strewn as a gesture of respect and welcome. The Buddhist monks undertook this journey on a new year to bless people.

If just the roads of Ayodhya were so beautiful, one only wonders how gorgeous the homes and palaces of Ayodhya must have been. In the next chapter, we will cover the buildings of Ayodhya and explore their beauty.

16

The Buildings of Ayodhya

According to Valmiki, the district of Ayodhya was surrounded with arched outer gateways and the front yards of buildings were well-laid out. The district housed all kinds of machinery, weaponry and craftsmen, and had well-arranged local markets.

The densly populated *purii* of Ayodhya had outstanding homes. The houses were of various sizes— large, medium and small—and were beautiful and gold-plated. Valmiki states in a *shloka*, 'It (Ayodhya) was bewitching, beautiful gold-plated homes, full of groups of excellent men and women adorned Ayodhya. The homes were also completely studded with all types of gemstones and were seven-storey high.' The word used for seven storeys is *vimaana*. We will discuss this word in the later chapters.

चित्रम् अष्टापद आकाराम् वर नारी गणैर् युताम् |
सर्व रत्न समाकीर्णाम् विमान गृह शोभिताम् || १-५-१६

*chiraam aSTaapada aakaaraam vara narii gaNaiH
yutaam |
sarva ratna samaakiirNaam vimaana gR^iha
shobhitaam || 1-5-16*

The word that Valmiki uses for describing homes in Ayodhya is *chitraam aSTaapada aakaaraam*, which translates to 'beautiful eight-stepped colour'. Certain commentators have translated it as a 'beautiful eight-legged shape'. The word *aSTaapada-aakaaraa* is different from *aSTaapaada-aakaaraa*, which means 'eight-legged'. This is a minor difference of the vowel 'aa' that is overlooked by many translators.

The word अष्टापद (*aSTaapada*) means 'eight steps'. In the dictionary, the process of gold plating is called *aSTaapada* because it takes eight steps to plate gold. Gold itself is also called *aSTapada*. This word is also used to describe 'heaven' and the 'Himalayas' because in order to climb the mountain range, one has to cross eight other mountains, as mentioned in Hindu and Jain scriptures.

Often, 'gold or gold coloured' is confused with अष्टापाद-आकारा (*aSTaapaada-aakaaraa*), which means a 'spider' or even a 'pregnant four-legged mammal', as a pregnant animal would be carrying four more legs inside its womb. In this word, there is an extra 'a' or 'aa' sound with '*paada*. In Sanskrit, *pada* means 'steps' and *paada* means 'legs'. For this reason, this is also incorrectly referred to as *aSTapadi* or *shariphal* or *dyutphalak*, which are boards on which you play ludo, chess and *pachisi* or *chausar*. All these games have a combination of either eight squares or eight moves to play. All three games: ludo, chess and *pachisi* or *chausar* were invented by ancient Hindus and have been extremely popular with the masses since ancient times.

Condiser the following images of a *pachisi* by Micha
Rieser and a chess board by ILA-boy, both on Wikipedia.
Notice the eight squares on each board.

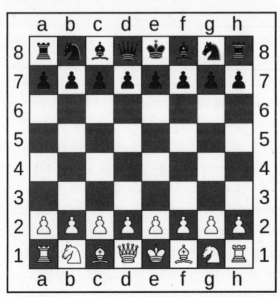

The word *aakaaraam* used with *aSTaapada* means both 'shape' and 'colour'. Ideally, after describing the layout and roadways of Ayodhya itself, there was no need to compare the 'shape' of the district again in the layout of a board game. Also, if you split the layout of the district with four highways, which join at the centre (but do not cross the centre), you get the shape of an irregular dice board, unlike that of ludo and *chausar*. These translations do not match with the dimensions of Ayodhya because it was 12 *yojanas* in length and 3 *yojanas* in width. For the dice board layout of Ayodhya to be correct, it had to be a square district and not a rectangular one. Therefore, the Gita Press Valmiki Ramayana gives the correct translation of *chitraam aSTaapada aakaaraam* as 'beautiful gold-coloured homes'.

Sage Valmiki, greatly skilled at using similar sounding words to mean different things, regularly creates mystery in the mind of the reader. However, to further confirm that Valmiki is talking of gold by using the word *aSTaapada aakaaraam*, it is crucial to mention that the concept of gold plating is still alive in Hindu culture. It is a sacred act that is now reserved for temples, though back in the day, in Ayodhya, buildings used to be covered in gold.

Hindu temples and homes were not only covered in gold but also contained huge amounts of the metal and other precious artifacts inside them. It is no secret that India was invaded repeatedly by Islamic rulers to loot its wealth, specifically temple gold. Interestingly, one just has to take a look at the numerous temples of India to know why she used to be called *sone ki chidia* (the golden bird) in the past.

To illustrate the same concept of gold plating, images of two temples of Bharat are shared. The one below, by user lovedeepsingh on Wikipedia, is of the Golden Temple in Amritsar, Punjab.

Next is the image of the complex of the Golden Temple of Vellore, inside Sripuram Spiritual Park. It is the temple of Goddess Sri Lakshmi Narayani or Maha Lakshmi, the Goddess of wealth. It is said that the Sripuram Golden Temple of Vellore is gilded with 1,500 kg of pure gold. This is double the amount used to gild the dome of the Golden Temple in Amritsar. The following image is captured by user Dsudhakar555 on Wikipedia.

Incidentally, the practice of gold plating temples and even homes was a common practice around the world. Before the Europeans invaded and looted the ancient Latin American cultures, gold plated buildings could be spotted all around. A sad example of the denuding of gold from temple walls by European invaders is of the South American country of Peru. In Peru, temples and other major places had gold plates covering the walls. But the gold was stripped and melted, made into bars and bricks and transported to Europe.

In Egypt, excavations of King Tutankhamun's tomb revealed it to be full of gold. His body was covered in a gold casket. His tomb was the only one found intact amongst all tombs from the Valley of the Kings and the Valley of the Queens. All other tombs were looted by raiders. Both these valleys housed numerous tombs, which contained gold caskets and precious belongings of the pharaohs. While none of these beautiful ancient cultures has survived the onslaught of Abrahmic cultures, the Hindu culture is the oldest and the last surviving indegenous culture in the world that still practices real gold plating on temples. For Hindus and the cultures influenced by Hindu thought, gold is auspisious and not just a precious metal.

To illustrate the example of ancient indigenous cultures using gold extensively in their temples and important places, the following image of a Peruvian gold wall has been shared. The image, captured by Manuel González Olaechea on Wikipedia, shows a thick gold wall cladding. These gold wall claddings once covered the now bare stone walls of the numerous ancient temples of Peru.

This image of gold cladding is from the private collection of Miguel Mujica Gallo, who later donated it to the state of Peru. It is housed in the Gold Museum of Peru and Weapons of the World, which is located in the district of Santiago de Surco, Lima.

Unlike the Hindus who value gold more than silver, Peruvians viewed both as equal. Therefore, the Peruvian temple walls or the exterior walls of homes were clad in both. For the Peruvian, pre-Inca civilisations, these metals represented the sun–moon, day–night, male–female duality and, hence, their use was ubiquitous in their cultural symbolism.

Another example of such elaborately designed and carved gold-cladded walls is a solid gold disc, the size of a wagon wheel, representing the Sun God from the magnificent temple of Koricancha in Cusco. Apart from the gold disk, many idols, the size of humans, with gold and silver life-size llamas were also discovered there. Previously, many such gold and silver metal plates covered the walls of the temple. The following image is obtained from the site yogoyo.com.

The motif in the gold disk belongs to the era prior to the Christians coming to South America, but today, it hangs on the outside walls of a church. The city of Cusco, where the disk is exhibited, was an important centre of indigenous people. It was the capital of the Inca Empire from the 13th until the 16th century, prior to the Spanish conquest. The Constitution of Peru designates Cusco as the historical capital of Peru. This ancient capital still follows certain traditions that date back to the pre-Inca times. On New Year's Day, as the clock strikes 12, Peruvian locals perambulate the town centre of Cuzco about seven times for good luck. These traditions are very similar to Hindus circumambulating the *garbha griha* (sanctum sanctorum) of temples as a mark of respect and reverence.

I have shared these examples for illustrative purposes, so that a reader can envision the houses of Ayodhya. A little part of the indigenous story is shared so that the reader is able to understand that gold plating or cladding was a rather common practice for all wealthy cultures of the past. Latin America was one of the last bastions of indigenous cultures that was totally decimated by the so-called 'discovery of America' and the arrival of the Europeans.

Since, along with Ayodhya, many other cultures also used gold on their buildings, Valmiki's description of gold-cladded walls in Ayodhya is not only accurate but also true.

17

The Shape and Structure of Residences

Along with *Vastu Shastra*, the science of town planning is expounded in various *shastras* like the *Shilpa Shastra*, *Niti Shastra* and *Smriti Shastra*. These *shastras* consist of explicit directions regarding town planning and selection of sites, and contain the minutest details of construction and beautification of all types of structures.

The details given in the science of engineering and construction in ancient Bharat dates back to antiquity. There are numerous references to the art of building in the *Rig Veda*, the *Atharva Veda* and the *Yajur Veda*. Hindu sages of ancient Bharat have described these sciences in detail in the various Puranas too, such as the *Agni Purana* and *Matsya Purana*. This science is also mentioned in the *Samhitas*. These ancient Hindu scientists called rishis have written a branch of the Veda known as *Shilpa Upaveda*. All these predate the Ramayanic Era and, therefore, it is no wonder that, based on all this knowledge, a beautiful city like Ayodhya could be constructed in Treta Yuga. The *Matsya Purana*, incidentally, contains the story of Manu whose descendants are Maharaja Dasharatha and Lord Rama.

The most important *shastra*, however, is by Manasara. It is said that he was a sage, but in Sanskrit, the term *manasara* itself means the 'essence of measurement'. The word is a conjunction of two Sanskrit words, which have the same meaning in Hindi too. They are pronounced in Sanskrit as *maana* and *saara*, where *saara* means 'essence'. Here, the word *maana* is not just an ordinary term meaning 'measurement'. It is actually a sacred term of measurement that pervades the cosmos.

It is said that everything in the cosmos is constructed according to defined ratios of *maana*, including planets, the heavens (darkness or space) and all natural elements, both animate and inanimate. Both the animate and inanimate elements, with their unique ratios of *maana*, are equally sacred, as they reverberate with inner energy. Often, this energy is identified as atoms in modern science and its study comes under the branch of physics. This reverberating energy is intelligent and is a function of *param tatva* or 'all pervading matter' spread throughout the cosmos. *Param tatva* is a part of *param aatma* or the 'all pervading consciousness or soul' of the cosmos.

Modern science today is able to calculate the distance between the Earth and the Sun, the speed of Earth's rotation on its axis and its rotation around the Sun. Based on these measurements, it then attempts to deduce justifications as to why only Earth has life and not other planets in the solar system. Very few scientists question who decided these particular measurements, ratios or *maana* and how they came into being in the first place. While modern science still has not found the centre of the cosmos around which our solar system revolves, ancient Hindu scientists, physicists and mathematicians have spoken about this centre, these sacred ratios or *maana*, and the *tatva* (matter) and *aatma* (consciousness) that pervades the cosmos.

Since energy can neither be created nor destroyed and it only transforms, Hindus consider *tatva*—to which both animate and inanimate elements belong—as intelligent. All life forms like birds, fishes, animals and humans, etc., are considered animate natural elements and the earth, space, fire, mountains and rivers, etc., are thought of as inanimate natural elements with the potential to give birth to life (animate forms) provided the conditions are right.

In many cultures, the inanimate is often regarded as non life-giving matter, with only a physical aspect. This is because human senses cannot perceive its non-physical aspects. Hindu *shastras* believe that all inanimate natural elements contain the possibility of life and this information is encoded in its non-physical aspects. It is the physical aspect that can be calculated in *maana* and this *maana* is mirrored in *Vaastu Shastra* to yield potential. Also, the inanimate always preceeds the animate.

It is believed that over a period of time, the energies of the inanimate combine to enable the possibility of creating the animate. Before animated life appeared on Earth, the planet, with its gushing rivers and majestic mountains, contained within it potential. It was pregnant with the potential of life, which arrived as certain conditions were met—just as a baby is born after a long period of incubation and the meeting of specific conditions. And for Earth to be born, the solar system had to first appear in the cosmos.

The same philosophy of transmutation of energies is behind the immense attention to detail in the Hindu *shastras* govering town planning, construction of homes and temples. In order to give birth to the innumerable unexhibited potentials of animate beings, the inanimate is constructed according to the defined ratios of *maana* existing in the cosmos, the solar system and on Earth.

Therefore, everything in Ayodhya is made in accordance with the principles of Manasara: from the layout of the district and roads to the architecture of buildings and palaces. Each followed explicit directions regarding town planning, selection of sites and the minute statements of mathematical proportions that particular type of construction was required to have. Another Sage Maya who contributed to *Vastu Shastra* and *Shilpa Shastra* is also mentioned in the Valmiki Ramayana as having constructed the altars for Emperor Dasharatha. In the next section, we will discuss exactly how proportionate Ayodhya was and also whether other ancient towns followed the layout proportions given by Manasara or not.

How Proportionate Were the Ancient Towns of Bharat?

There are five basic principles on which *Vastu Shastra* stands. The first and second principles are with regards to the orientation and the layout of the plot. 'Proportionate measurements' or *maana* is the third fundamental principle of the ancient Hindu practice of *Vastu Shastra*. The fourth and fifth principles are related to the components of the building and its aesthetics. The adherence to *maana* is an integral part of the science of Hindu architecture and imperative to all creative activity.

While we do not have much archeological proof that defines the boundaries of Ayodhya, apart from the dug-up ruins of the Ram Janmabhoomi Temple, we do have data from Dholavira. Dholavira's example can be taken to deduce and imagine the proportions of the capital district of Ayodhya and its structure. These examples are produced to prove that Manasara's *maanas* were followed diligently by all ancient Hindu town planners and constructors. The image of the layout of Dholavira has already been included in Part II of this book and is being reshared here.

Dholavira is the largest excavated Harappan site till date, in India. What makes it unique is the fact that it was a continuous settlement for over 1,700 years and was most likely abandoned due to harsh environmental factors. Dholavira is considered to be a part of the Saraswati-Sindhu Civilisation of Bharat.

Dholavira's elaborate town planning was based on the conscious use of specific proportions for various enclosures. An article by *Frontline* magazine titled 'The Rise and Fall of a Harappan City' by T.S. Subramanian, quotes Lt L.S. Bisht, a Sanskrit scholar and an Indian archaeologist known for his scholarship on the Indus Valley Civilisation, another name for the Saraswati-Sindhu Civilisation. The excerpt of that article is given below.

Lt Bisht says about Dholavira, 'The city of Dholavira in its fullest form was a precisely proportionate whole

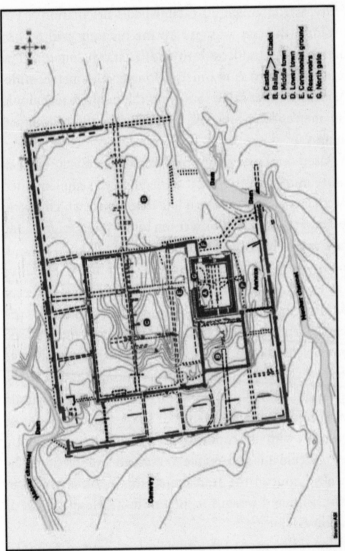

The Layout of Dholavira

and a proportionately resolved configuration, which followed a resolute set of principles of planning and architecture with mathematical precision and perhaps with astronomically established orientation. For instance, the city was 711.10 metres long and 616.87 metres wide, the length to width ratio being 5:4. The castle internal was 114 metres long and 92 metres wide, maintaining the same ratio, and the castle external was 151 metres long and 118 metres wide, the ratio again being 5:4.'

Based on the evidence provided by Lt Bisht, one can pretty much assume that if such detail was implemented for an inconspicuous town like Dholavira, which has no record in Hindu oral or written history, how rigorously they would have been practised in Ayodhya.

Just like Dholavira, the town planning of Ayodhya was based on the conscious use of specific proportions. Ayodhya had a 4:1 ratio. 12 *yojanas*:3 *yojanas* = 4:1 *yojanas* ratio. The capital district of Ayodhya and the palaces should have had the same ratio—just like Dholavira's corresponding proportionate ratio for the castle and its city boundaries. And hence, when Valmiki keeps reiterating the beauty of shapes and divisions of Ayodhya with its proportionate buildings, how accurate he is. While it is impossible to recreate the splendour he speaks about in the Ramayana, this book attempts to share as many images to illustrate his descriptions of Ayodhya.

The *shloka* used to describe the buildings of Ayodhya is mentioned in the *Bala Kanda, sarga* 5, *shloka* 19. The astute Valmiki says, 'Like an aerial car/space station acquired by the *Siddhas* in heaven through their austerities, the palaces were perfectly constructed in rows and inhabited by the noblest of men.' Here, he portrays that these evenly constructed, well planned palaces are beautiful inside and out, and are inhabited by the best quality of men and women. Because of these beautiful houses and people, he likens Ayodhya to a *vimaana* obtained by *Siddhas* for their austerities. The *vimaana* is what is translated as an 'aerial car' or even a 'space station' in certain places.

विमानम् इव सिद्धानाम् तपस अधिगतम् दिवि |
सु निवेशित वेश्मान्ताम् नरोत्तम समावृताम् ||१-५-१९

vimaanam iva siddhaanaam tapasa adhigatam divi |
su niveshita veshmaantam nara uttama sama
aavR^ittam || 1-5-19

A *siddha* in Hindu dharma means a master who has achieved a high degree of physical as well as spiritual perfection or enlightenment. Usually, a *siddha* by virtue of his *sadhna* has attained one or many *siddhis* or 'paranormal capabilities like changing matter, creating illusions, reversing their age, and moving back and forth in time'. *Sadhna* means a method or practice adopted to accomplish a specific goal. They are done to transform one's inner state to imitate the actions and experiences of a perfect being like the Supreme Lord Vishnu, Brahma or any other devi or *devata*.

Sage Valmiki does not bring about a similitude between Ayodhya and *vimaana* randomly. Previously, in another *shloka* from the same *sarga*, the erudite sage states that the palaces of the nobles were like *vimaana* itself. In *shloka* 16 from the same *sarga*, Valmiki describes by saying, 'It (Ayodhya) was bewitching, beautiful gold-plated homes, full of groups of excellent men and women adorned Ayodhya. The homes were also completely studded with all types of gemstones and were seven storeys high.' The word used for seven-storey is again *vimaana*. The *shloka* copy in Sanskrit is provided in the chapter titled, 'Buildings of Ayodhya'.

The use of the word *vimaana* is bewildering for a person who is unaware of Hindu culture and cosmology. Therefore, an attempt to solve this puzzle through examples cited in various books of architecture and Hindu cosmology is done in this book. But before that we will go over some images of a *vimaana* and understand what it actually means.

What Is a *Vimaana*?

The following images are illustrations of Ram Raz, who published these in his book, *Essay on the Architecture of the Hindus* by the Royal Asiatic Society of Great Britain and Ireland in 1834. Ram Raz was an Indian scholar who studied various *shastras* dealing with architecture, statue-making and construction to compile his book on Hindu architecture. This book contains numerous illustrations of various sizes of *vimaanas*. The first image shared is of a *vimaana* consisting of 5 storeys, followed by images of 2, 7 and 16 storeys.

Another Vimaana of Two Storeys

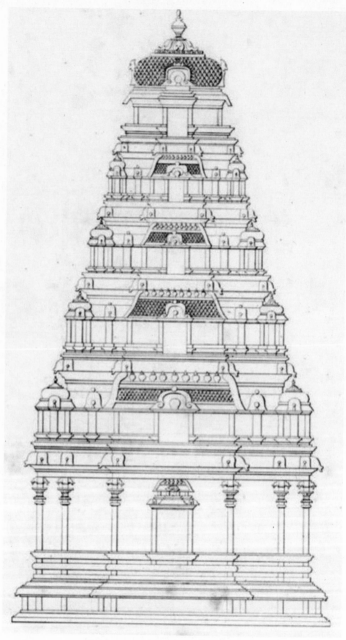

A Vimaana Consisting of Five Storeys

A Vimaana Consisting of Seven Storeys

One can easily find the similarities between these *vimaanas* and Hindu temples till date. Proper Hindu temples even today are constructed to the specifications laid out in *Shilpa Shatra* and *Vastu Shastra*. In South India, various versions of *vimaana*-style temples still stand tall, unlike in North India where they were demolished by Islamic invaders. In their place, hastily- and shabbily-built mosques were constructed, often with the same stones of the ruined temple. A well acknowledged example is the Babri Masjid that was constructed over the Ram Janmabhoomi Temple in the 16th century by the Mughal ruler Babur.

According to Ram Raz, a *vimaana* is a pyramidal structure. He explains the same in his book *Essay on the Architecture of the Hindus* with an excerpt from the Valmiki Ramayana (which I have shared earlier) and by using examples from *Manasara*. An exact image of the book containing the same description is shared below.

kettle-drums, tabors, cymbals, and lutes; this city truly surpassed any that was ever beheld on earth. The houses which it contained resembled the celestial mansions which the *Sidd'hás* obtain through the virtue of their austerity."

Of the remaining portion of the *Mánásara*, twelve successive chapters, from the eighteenth to the twenty-ninth, are entirely taken up with rules respecting the measurements, &c. of as many sorts of *vimánas* or pyramidal temples. The same subject is also treated of in several sections of the *Cásyapa*.

" A *vimána* consists, according to the former, ' of from one to twelve stories;' and according to the latter, ' of from one to sixteen stories;' and ' is made round, quadrangular, or of six or eight sides.' The form of the edifice may be uniformly the same from the basement up to the spire, whether it be square, oblong, circular, oval, or the like; or it may be of a mixed nature, composed partly of one and partly of another form.' " " A

Interestingly, these beautiful and symmetrical *vimaanas* are a replica of an even more ancient object mentioned in Hindu scriptures and cosmology. They are not the original design of Manasara or any other *Shilpa Shastra* engineer or author, but rather a mimicry of another mysterious and exotic object created by Brahma himself. Can you guess what the original *vimaana* was?

What Was the Original *Vimaana*?

Various Hindu scriptures contain numerous references to *vimaanas*. Most of these are referred to as 'aerial chariots' or 'aerial cars' used by the Gods. Some have even called them 'aerial space stations'. According to *Samarangana Sutradhara*, a treatise on *Vastu Shastra* containing details of classical Indian architecture written by Paramara King Bhoja, it was Brahma who created the first five prime *vimaanas* for the Gods. They were:

Vairaja for himself, Brahma (the creator)
Kailasa for Shiva (the destroyer)
Pushpaka for Kubera (the banker of the Gods)
Manika for Varuna (the lord of the sky and the ocean)
Trivistapa for Vishnu (the preserver)

The corresponding *shlokas* are in the 49th chapter of the *Samarangana Sutradhara* and are given below. The translation is: 'In the ancient time, Brahma created five *vimaanas* or aircrafts for the *suras* or Gods, which could traverse the sky and darkness (the vast space). These *shrImanti* (beautiful, famous, glorious) and *mahAnti* (invulnerable) *vimaanas* were Trivistapa, Manika, Vairaja, Pushpaka and Kailasa. They were golden, beautiful and studded with gems.

पुरा ब्रह्मासृजत् पञ्च विमनान्यसुरद्विषम् ।
वियद्वर्त्मविचारीणि श्रीमन्ति च महान्ति च ॥

तानि वैराजकैलासे पुष्पाकं मणिकाभिधम् ।
हैमानि मणिचित्राणि पञ्चमं च त्रिविष्टपम् ॥

*purA brahmAsRRijat pa~ncha
vimanAnyasuradviSham |
viyadvartmavichArINi shrImanti cha mahAnti cha | |*

*tAni vairAjakailAse puShpAkaM maNikAbhidham |
haimAni maNichitrANi pa~nchamaM cha
triviShTapam | |*

Later on, inspired by these five shapes, architects designed the *prasada* or palace/residences/temples. These *prasadas* were to be built in towns and are made of stone, burnt bricks or iron. As time passed, there were additions to the original designs of *vimaanas*.

In the Ramayana, Sage Valmiki states that the homes of the citizens of Ayodhya were like *vimaanas*, studded with all types of precious gemstones. While Manasara mentions that the private houses of residents should have one to twelve storeys, depending on the rank of the person, the word *vimaana* is usually translated to 'a palace or house with seven storeys'. Various commentators, too, have mentioned that the homes of the citizens of Ayodhya were seven-storey tall. This is because the various Sanskrit dictionaries, including that of Vaaman Shivram Apte, carry this definition from certain *nighaNTus*. A *nighaNTu* in Sanskrit is a work that has a collection of words grouped into certain categories. The words in these collections contain added explanations and comments.

Apte quotes *vimaana* as 'a palace (with seven storeys); विमानोऽस्त्री देवयाने सप्तभूमौ च सद्मनि इति निघण्टुः'. Here, there is a correction to be made in the first word, which has been corrected and written as following.

विमानः अस्ति देवयाने सप्तभूमौ च सद्मनि इति निघण्टुः

vimAnaH asti devayAne saptabhUmau cha sadmani iti nighaNTuH:

The *nighaNTu* clearly states that *vimaanas* are vehicles of the gods and the above line loosely translates to '*vimaanas* are the vehicles of the devas in which there are seven earths and a palace (dwelling atop)'.

In the mega epic Ramayana, the *vimaana* or aerial chariot of Kubera was captured by Ravana. Ravana had defeated his stepbrother Kubera and driven him out of Lanka. It is in this *Pushpaka Vimaana* of Kuber, that Ravana abducts Devi Sita, a reincarnation of Goddess Lakshmi, and carries her to his castle.

Whereas one could debate whether the palaces of Ayodhya had 7, 12 or 16 floors, all scriptures clearly state that *vimaanas* were the flying vehicles of *devatas*. These *vimaanas* were of various shapes and sizes. The closest we can get to deciphering *vimaanas* is to go by the descriptions mentioned in the *Vimanika Shastra*.

Four main types of flying *vimaanas* described in it are: *Rukma, Sundara, Tripura and Sakuna*. The *Rukmas* were conical in shape and dyed gold, whereas the *Sundaras* were like rockets and had a silver sheen. The *Tripuras* were three-storeyed and the *Sakunas* looked like birds. The *Pushpaka Vimaana* of Kuber was a *Sakuna Vimaana*.

Images of these *vimaanas* were drawn by T.K. Ellapa under the instructions of Pandit Subbaraya Sastry, a mystic from Anekal, India. Below are the illustrations of two of these: the *Rukma* and *Sundara*. One cannot ignore the uncanny inspiration found in the pyramidal shapes of both the aerial chariots and the buildings based on the principles of *Vastu Shastra*.

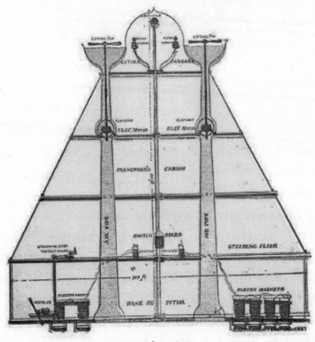

Vertical section
Rukma Vimaana

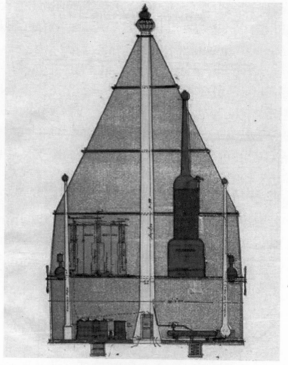

Vertical section
Sundara Vimaana

These images are given as a guide to show how the
inspiration behind the pyramidal shape of the *vimaana*-
like homes and palaces of Ayodhya were based on the
shapes of aerial chariots.

Curiously enough, non aerial chariots, too, had
pyramidal or conical shape. An example of such a
chariot is at the National Museum of India in New
Delhi. The chariot is an inverse octagonal pyramid.
Though this image is only half of the chariot, one can
observe how it is narrower at the base and broader
at the top. This is a temple chariot dedicated to Lord

Vishnu, made of Sal and Sagwan wood. It has 5 tiers consisting of 6 wheels, beams, 425 carved panels, brackets, angles, etc., weighing approximately 2,200 kg. This 18th- or 19th-century chariot has been on display since December 2003 at the museum's entrance. The image below has been captured by G. Katyan Misra. Since the chariot is caged in a glass box, it looks a bit hazy. On the right of the chariot is an inverse octagonal pyramid for comparison. The image of the octagonal pyramid is by user Jolly Monkey, uploaded on Flickr.

Another image of a chariot from The National Handicrafts and Handlooms Museum in New Delhi is shared next. It is one of the largest crafts museums in the country. This image is captured by Anil Bhardwaj, Noida. Here, too, one can observe the pyramidal shape over the chariot.

Numerous people have claimed that the mechanics behind flying machines covered in *Vimanika Shastra* is pseudoscience. It is laughable that they have come to this conclusion without adequate help of *samhitas* and *sutras*, which carry innumerable detailed information describing the workings of the *shastra*. No *shastra* in Hindu literature can be interpreted literally. Often, there are words with dual meanings that are meant to confuse and mislead the reader. It was done to prevent knowledge from falling into the hands of those who do not come from the guru–shishya *parampara* (teacher–student tradition).

These *shastras* only cover encoded information considered to be tips for a person who is well-versed in its science. This science is only taught by a guru to a shishya. A perfect example of it is *Patanjali Yoga Sutra*. Patanjali is the genius behind yoga. Curiously, it does not contain all the detailed postures called asanas that yoga is famous for today. The postures and other details are mentioned in numerous other s*amhitas* like the *Gheranda Samhita, Hatha Yoga Pradipika* and various other treatises of yoga. Sage Patanjali expects you to have mastered them before graduating to his treatise.

The example of *Patanjali Yoga Sutra* is given so that the reader understands that the texts leading to the *Vimanika Shastra* have been lost to mankind and the guru–shishya transfer of knowledge has been broken for this particular stream of science. Interestingly, the word 'science' in Sanskrit is called विज्ञान (vij~nAna), which is described in Sanskrit as 'knowldege that is studied in a special/minute/detailed manner'.

विशेष रूपेण ज्ञायते इति विज्ञानं
visheSha rUpeNa j~nAyate iti vij~nAnaM

This meaning is attributed to the word विज्ञान because of the prefix वि (vi) before the Sanskrit word ज्ञान (*j~nAna*), which means knowledge. Applying the same वि (*vi*) prefix before मान (*maana*), we can also derive the word विमान (*vimaana*), which would mean 'measurement that is specially minute/detailed'. As explained previously, the word *maana* is not just an ordinary term meaning 'measurement'. It is a sacred term of measurement that pervades the cosmos. The ratios of *maana* are derived from the ratios that exist in the cosmos, like those between heavenly bodies, specifically life-giving heavenly bodies, their orientation, their rotations and their effects on each other (gravitation), etc.

Having stated this, one is acutely aware that any aircraft or satellite, unless it is designed with specially-detailed measurements, can never lift off or posess the ability to fly. In addition, in order to be a flying machine, it needs to be aerodynamic. And, aerodynamic measurements include measurements of forces that act on the surface of a solid body relative to which the motion takes place. These include the measurements of velocity, pressure, density, temperature of moving air and heat transfer to the surface as well. All these require detailed, minute and specialised knowledge.

Because in the past, various ancient indigenous cultures utilised the measurement of *vimaanas* (encompassing the measurements of forces and movements acting on its surface), we still see ancient monuments standing the test of time as we continue to be hurled across space on a rotating mass called planet Earth. These monuments spread across the earth, built by ancient men, can be observed mimmicing the pyramidal *vimaanas* as shown in the images above. Since this shape is extremely sacred to all ancient indigenous traditions, they are found from tombs to temples and from the Great Pyramids of Giza in Egypt to the Great Pyramid of Cholula in Mexico.

Following is the artwork of David Roberts from Rawpixel. He has drawn the Pyramids of Egypt beautifully.

Below is an image of the Grand Pyramid of Cholula captured by Diego Delso. It is the largest pyramid by volume known to exist in the world today, twice the size of the pyramids at Giza. This pyramid is a temple dedicated to God Quetzalcoatl, a feathered serpent god.

There are many other ancient cultures that considered the pyramidal structure sacred. Examples of two pyramids from different continents and cultures have been shared to emphasise the continuity of cultural traditions and the common heritage and values these cultures shared with Hindus. They shared the same philosophy in terms of sacredness of the pyramidal structure and systematically adhered to the five basic principles of *Vaastu Shastra*. Despite various onslaughts on Hindus, they have maintained the continuity of knowledge that states the inspiration behind the pyramidal structures were the original aerial chariots/space stations created by Lord Brahma, while other cultures succumbed to invasions and lost their cultural continuity.

As these ancient cultures died, their knowledge systems perished with them and in the process, this science was lost to 'modernised' cultures. Many Western archeologists and Egyptiologists have expressed bewilderment as to why and how the pyramids of Giza are pointing to the true north. This particular orientation of a structure is covered under the first principle of *Vaastu Shastra* and is faithfully adhered to by the Hindus since ancient times. Therefore, homes constructed with a north orientation always carried a premium and even today, the price of such a residential home in New Delhi is higher compared to one that does not comply to this principle. Homes following all the five principles are labelled as 'Vaastu-compliant' and are much sought after.

Now that we have covered the basics of *Vaastu Shastra*, the shapes of *vimaanas* and the inspiration behind the pyramydial structures, we will discuss the palaces mentioned in the Ramayana.

18

The Palaces of Ayodhya

One generally assumes that only the emperor or the king residing in a city will have his own palace. But it is unlikely that there is just one palace in a city in ancient India. Many rich people also lived in large palaces, just like they do in palatial homes today. Valmiki acknowledges the presence of numerous palaces in Ayodhya.

In Ayodhya, the palaces were very large and almost touched the sky. Like the homes of other citizens, they were pyramidal in structure and gold plated. Sage Valmiki observes the following about the palaces of Ayodhya, 'Palaces are ornamentally studded with precious gems and as high as mountains, and filled with them she is like *Amaravati*, the capital of Indra.'

प्रासादै रत्न विकृतैः पर्वतैः इव शोभिताम् ।
कूटागारैः च संपूर्णाम् इन्द्रस्य इव अमरावतीम् ।१-५-१५

*praasadaiH ratna vikR^itaiH parvataiH iva
upashobhitaam |
kuuTagaraiH cha sampuurNaam indrasya iva
amaraavatiim || 1-5-15*

Palaces as high as mountains would translate to multi-storeyed skyscrapers today. Below is an image of the K2 mountain, which is part of the Karakoram mountain range. This image is to show why Valmiki says that the palaces look like mountains in Ayodhya. Pay attention to the pyramidal shape and the towering height of the mountain. This image has been captured by svy123 and uploaded on Wikipedia.

Compare the image of K2 with the image of a typical structure of a South Indian temple *gopuram*, such as the one from the Srirangam Temple, clicked by user Sowriranjan, Wikipedia. Notice the similarities in shape and the gradual narrowing structure of the peak.

A *gopuram* is an ornate and grand entrance tower at the entrance of a Hindu temple. A temple can have more than one *gopuram*. With the examples of the images above, the reader must now have a clear idea of why Valmiki says the palaces are *parvataiH iva upashobhitaam*, which means 'palaces looking like mountains, and (therefore) beautifully adorning the *nagarii* of Ayodhya'.

Shared next is a beautifully lit up temple complex of the Tiruvannamalai Temple complex, Tamil Nadu, captured by Suresh and uploaded on Wikipedia. It seems to have been taken on a Diwali night when the city is lit up. Here, one can easily judge the imposing height of this gorgeous temple shining bright at night. The temple has four *gopurams*, with the main one appearing to be the tallest.

With the image of this temple, surely the reader will be able to comprehend why the palaces stood out like mountains and adorned the *nagarii* of Ayodhya. Bear in mind that the rest of the houses of Ayodhya have an average of seven storeys. In this image, one can see a stark difference between the height of the houses in the rest of the city and the majestic *gopurams* of this stunning temple.

In the same *shloka*, Valmiki states that the palaces were ornamentally studded with gems. The tradition of intricately decorating homes and palaces with gemstones dates back to antiquity in India. This art was adapted by invaders who came to India as well. A prime example of this is the Taj Mahal in Agra. This sort of inlay work is popular in homes even today across various states of India. Most inlay work is now done in marble, though only a few homes use real gemstones.

Embellishing with gold and gems would come under the fifth principle of *Vaastu,* which is concerned with aesthetics. This, too, was a normal cultural practice of many ancient civilisations like the pre-Incan and ancient Egyptian. Today, only a few cultures retain their adherence to this principle. The Thai rulers have done a fabulous job of adorning walls of palaces and temples with gold, inlaid with precious stones. These days, however, real gold has been replaced with gold colour.

The reader can find below an image of the dazzling Wat Phra Kaew Temple. This temple is located within the grounds of the Wat Phra Kaew Grand Palace, Bangkok, Thailand. It is enshrined with a revered idol of Lord Buddha, which has been meticulously and intricately carved out from a single block of jade.

The golden coloured temple, also called the Temple of the Emerald Buddha, intricately studded with coloured stones and coloured glass from top to bottom, is just spellbinding. In Treta Yuga, instead of using coloured glasses and stones, real gemstones were used. That is why Valmiki, throughout the Ramayana, keeps using adjectives, such as shining bright, gleaming, glowing, bright and beautiful, to describe Ayodhya's palaces, and keeps comparing them to the sun and the moon, as these two are the brightest visible objects in the sky.

Standing in front of this beautiful temple of the ruling Chakri dynasty of Thailand are two golden coloured gatekeepers, or *dwarapalas* as they are called in Sanskrit. Observe the pyramidal structure at the top of the building as well as on the door of the temple. The image below shows a similar peak on top of the temple—a facet of all ancient cultures. This temple complex satisfies various *Vastu Shastra* and *Shilpa Shastra* design elements like the *dwarapala*, and the gold covering on the walls and the pillars. The measured and phased pyramidal narrowing of the top of the temple is not clearly accentuated in the image, though this design of an elongated top portion of the shrine is commonly observed in newer temples.

The Royal Wat Phra Kaew Temple in Bangkok is used for various religious ceremonies by the country's royal family. Their reigning monarch, King Maha Vajiralongkorn, is officially called King Rama X and belongs to the Chakri Dynasty. Close to Bangkok lies the city of Ayutthya (Ayodhya), an older capital of Thailand. Bangkok, the new capital, was established by Rama I, the first king of the Chakri Dynasty post the destruction of Ayutthya by the Burmese army in 1767.

King Phra Buddha Yotfa Chulalok, officially titled King Rama I, decided to name his dynasty Chakri, in reference to the chakra (discus) of Vishnu. The emblem of the Chakri dynasty is a chakra intersecting with Shiva's *trisula* (trident) and its image is shared below.

A delightful expression of the ancient historical and civilisational relationship between Bharat and Thailand is documented on the website of the Royal Embassy of Thailand in India. The site states 'The relationship between Thailand and India is deep-rooted, long-standing and multidimensional, ranging from the ties among the peoples, governments, armed forces, businesses, scholars and educators, to the bond India has had with the Thai Monarchy. The link goes back centuries. The very concept of Thai Kingship itself has been greatly influenced by Buddhist and Brahmin philosophies, and one can still notice Indian cultural traces in many ceremonies and rituals of the Royal Court Thailand to this day. Historically, Thai kings of various eras have always tried to follow the Buddhist ideal of the "Ten Virtues (or Dharmas) of Kingship" (*Dasabidh Raja Dham*). The traditional names of many ruling Thai kings at least since the period of the Ayutthaya Kingdom (1351–1767) was either "Ramesuan" or "Ramathibodi" (Rama the Ruler), and of course, the old capital city of Ayutthaya itself was named after Rama's city Ayodhya.'

King Rama I, with the help of Brahmins, scholars and poets, translated and composed the Thai version of the Ramayana called Ramakian or 'the honour of Rama' and the two-kilometre long walls of the Royal Wat Phra Kaew Temple are decorated in murals telling the story of Ramakian in its entirety. This temple is in the Grand Palace of Bangkok.

Apart from the description of gem-studded skyscraper palaces in Ayodhya, Valmiki specifically describes two important royal palaces as well. One is the palace of Empress Kaikeyi and the other of Prince Rama and Devi Sita. Can you visualise how the palaces must have looked like?

What Was Dasharatha and Kaikeyi's Palace Like?

Valmiki gives a beautiful and detailed description of the palace of Emperor Dasharatha and his Empress Kaikeyi, which looked like heaven with beautifully adorned women. Descriptions of the gorgeous palace are dotted along the path of Maharaja Dasharatha's movement in the palace as he searches for Kaikeyi.

Emperor Dasharatha had three main empresses, who are referred as *patta rani* in Hindu culture. He also had several other queens. A *patta rani* is the consort of a king who sits with him on the throne. She has equal powers to run the empire and her children are the rightful heirs to the throne. Other queens do not share the throne nor control the workings of the empire.

Kaushalya was the first consort, Kaikeyi was second and Sumitra the third. All three had the right to share the throne with him and run the empire with him or in his absence. Therefore, all three would be titled 'empress'. Each of these empresses were the mothers of four princes: Kaushalya was the mother of Prince Rama, Kaikeyi of Prince Bharata and Sumitra was the mother of Princes Lakshmana and Shatrughna. Empress Kaikeyi was the favourite consort of Maharaja Dasharatha. She wanted her son Bharata to inherit the throne, so she asked for Prince Rama to be banished for 14 years in lieu of two wishes owed to her by Dasharatha.

Sage Valmiki mentions the palace of Kaikeyi in detail when Emperor Dasharatha enters his *antaH puram*, which translates to 'the female apartments of a king's place'. In this section, it probably implies Empress Kaikeyi's palace's inner apartments. Some commentators have not separated the palace as being hers or his. They have quoted it as 'the' palace, though in the following *shloka* from *sarga* 7 of *Ayodhya Kanda*, Kaikeyi's palace is specifically described as shining like a full moon in the sky.

ज्ञातिदासी यतो जाता कैकेय्या तु सहोषिता |
प्रासादं चन्द्रसङ्काशमारुरोह यदृच्छया || २-७-१

GYaatidaasi yataH jaataa kaikeyyaa tu saha
ushhitaa |
praasaadam chandrasa~Nkaasham aaruroha
yadR^ichchhayaa || 2-7-1

The exact translation of this *shloka* is as follows, 'Manthara, a housemaid who was residing with Kaikeyi since her birth, accidentally ascended the balcony/ attic of Kaikeyi's white palace which resembled the full moon.'

In *sarga* 10, Dasharatha comes looking for Kaikeyi and enters the *antaH puram*. The literal translation of the *shloka* is, 'Dasharatha entered his (queen's) magnificent palace but could not find his beloved Kaikeyi on her best couch there. Peacocks and parrots were being reared in that palace, sounds of birds like cranes or curlews and swans were heard around. The place was resonant with sounds of musical instruments.

Short and hunchbacked maid-servants were moving here and there. There were bowers surrounded by creepers and lovely Champaka and Ashoka trees. There were painted rooms. There were altars built with ivory, silver and gold. There were trees yielding flowers and fruits in all seasons and wells in the middle. There were beautiful seats constructed with ivory, silver and gold. Various types of food, drinks and snacks were made available. That palace looked like heaven with beautifully adorned women.'

शुकबर्हिणसंयुक्तं क्रौञ्चहंसरुतायुतम् || २-१०-१२
वादित्ररवसंघुष्टं कुब्जावामनिकायुतम् |
लतागृहैश्चित्रगृहैश्चम्पकाशोकशोभितैः || २-१०-१३
दान्तराजत सौवर्णवेदिकाभिस्समायुतम् |
नित्यपुष्पफलैर्वृक्षैर्वापीभिश्रोपशोभितम् || २-१०-१४
दान्तराजतसौवर्णैः संवृतं परमासनैः |
विविध्यैरत्नपानैश्च भक्ष्यैश्चिव विधैरपि || २-१०-१५
उपपन्नं महार्हैश्च भूषितैस्त्रिदिवोपमम् |
तत्प्रविश्य महाराजः स्वमन्तःपुरमृद्धिमत् || २-१०-१६
न ददर्श प्रियां राजा कैकेयीं शयनोत्तमे |

shukabarahiNa samyuktam krauncha hamsa
rutaayutam || 2-10-12
vaaditrarava sanghushhtam kubjaa vaamanikaayutam |
lataagR^ihaiH cha chitragR^ihaiH cha champaka
ashoka shobhitaiH || 2-10-13
daantaraajata souvarNa vedikaabhiH samaayutam |
nitya pushhpa phalaiH vR^ikshhaiH vaapiibhiH cha
upashobhitam ||2-10-14
daantaraajata sauvarNaiH samvR^itam
paramaasanaiH |

vividhaiH annapaanaiH cha bhakshhaiH cha
vividhaiH api || 2-10-15
upapannam mahaarhaiH cha bhuushhitaiH
stridivopamam |
tat pravishya mahaaraajaH svam antaH puram
Riddhimat || 2-10-16
nadadarsha priyam raajaa kaikeyiim shayauottame |

The palace was magnificently abundant in things of
beauty. Valmiki talks of *lataagR^ihaiH*, which translates
to 'bowers surrounded with creepers'. A bower is a
pleasant shady place under trees or under climbing
plants in a garden or in the woods. Often, bowers are
made for birds to nest there. In the *shloka*, Valmiki says
that they were homes for creepers. The image below by
Caio Resende is a sample of a 'bower for creepers'. In
this picture, the bower is over a pathway.

Apart from pathways, bowers used to be made over
seats, too, so that one could sit snugly under the shadow

of creepers and the sweet smelling flowers, just like in the picture below, titled *Rustic Bower* sourced from The Metropolitan Museum of Art.

Rustic Bower

And here is an image of Lord Krishna and Radha under a bower, which is much smaller and cosier. This sort of a bower would be perfect for romance. In this image, one can clearly see the flower-laden creepers knitted over the bower. There are lovely flowering trees in the garden too. The night sky is resplendent with the moon and the stars shining above.

Valmiki further adds that there were *vedikas* built with ivory, silver and gold. It was difficult to get the exact idea of *vedikas*, as these had evolved quite a lot from the time of the *Rig Veda* by the time Treta Yuga came around.

Vedika is loosely translated to an altar. They are sacrificial fire altars or a raised ground for fire sacrifices. *Vedikas* are smaller than *vedis*, which, too, are sacrificial fire altars. Some *vedikas* are described as benches and pavilions as well.

Given below is a typical *vedi* of ancient times, from an era preceeding the Treta Yuga. These *vedis*, in use even today, are in the form of step pyramids and have a detatchable top portion used for worship by means of fire. The image is from krishnamall.com. This *vedi* also known as a *havan kund*.

Another meaning of *vedi* is a covered verandah or balcony in the courtyard. A quadrangular spot in the courtyard of a temple or palace, usually furnished with a raised floor or seat, and covered with a roof supported by pillars is also described as a *vedi* or a *vedika* in few Sanskrit dictionaries. When describing the garden and the frontal chambers of the palace, it can be assumed that it was a covered verandah in a courtyard, similar to a pavilion. Considering pavilions were very common in ancient India, especially in palace gardens, it is presumed that Sage Valmiki is referring to those. Also, Valmiki adds that there were beautiful seats constructed with ivory, silver and gold in the *vedikas* and the gardens. Below is an image of a white *sawan bhado* pavilion from the Red Fort, Delhi, by Hemant Banswal and uploaded on Wikipedia. The Hindi word for a *vedika* is *chabootra*.

Sage Valmiki further states that the garden had trees yielding flowers and fruits in all seasons and ponds in the middle. When speaking of the ponds and pools of the palace, he uses the Sanskrit term *vaapiibhiH*, which translates to 'many oblong ponds'. There were many oblong pools or ponds in Empress Kaikeyi's palace, such as the one captured below by Tom Fisk.

Nowadays, most people assume that lakes, ponds or pools were present in palaces for ornamental reasons. But they were used for multifarious activities, including supplying drinking water. Its *ghaats* (banks) were used for bathing and its depths to store jewels. Like the palaces of Ayodhya, other capitals, too, had numerous lakes. Interestingly, for this reason, Janakpur, the ancient capital city of Videha, is labelled the city of lakes and temples. This Nepalese city is a famous Hindu pilgrimage site and among its numerous temples is a grand temple called Janaki Mandir for Devi Sita, who is supposed to have grown up there. Devi Sita's father was Maharaja Janak and Janakpur in Sanskrit means the 'capital of Janak'. According to the oral legend, the wedding of Lord Rama and Devi Sita took place in Janakpur and since many distingushed guests and revered rishis participated in the celebrations, Maharaja Janak got numerous ponds and lakes dug for them in addition to the existing ones in the capital.

The *shloka* that speaks of the arrival of numerous rishis, sages and brahmins for the wedding is mentioned in the *Bala Kanda*, *sarga* 69. The *shloka* given below translates to: 'Providentially bechanced is the arrival of this great, resplendent and godly Sage Vashishta, who arrived here with all of these eminent Brahmans, like Indra himself with all gods.'

दिष्ट्या प्राप्तो महातेजा वसिष्ठो भगवान् ऋषिः || १-६९-१०
सह सर्वैः द्विज श्रेष्ठैः देवैः इव शतक्रतुः |

diShTyA prApto mahAtejA vasiShTho bhagavAn
RRiShiH || 1-69-10

saha sarvaiH dvija shreShThaiH devaiH iva
shatakratuH |

Even today, no pilgrimage in Janakpur is complete without a ritual bath in the Ganga Sagar Lake, which was filled by the holy waters of river Ganges. There are more than 70 sacred lakes and ponds in Janakpur, each with its own interesting story. Three such lakes are Bihar Kund, Angrag Sar and Ratna Sagar.

Towards the north of Janaki Mandir lies Angrag Sar or Aragaja, where a dip is known to cure skin diseases. According to the local legend, Devi Sita used to bathe in this pond after smearing her body with turmeric paste. Turmeric is popular amongst Hindus for its antibacterial, anti-inflammatory and antioxidant properties.

The water of Bihar Kund is so clean that people drink from it even in the present day. This lake used to be frequented by Devi Sita, her sisters and her friends for a bath, even after she was married to Lord Rama. Ratna Sagar is the lake where Maharaja Janak used to store his jewels. When observed from a corner, this mysterious lake appears to be red and after the *aarti* (a ritual offering of light to a deity) by the local temple priests, its red colour is said to disappear.

As Sage Valmiki describes the path of Emperor Dasharatha from the gardens to the inner chambers of Kaikeyi's palace, he moves from describing the gardens and lakes to the details of the palace. In the inner portions of the palace, there were *chitragR^ihaiH* or 'rooms with paintings'. This could also be translated as 'beautiful rooms', as the Sanskrit word *chitra* means 'variegated, colourful and beautiful' as well as 'paintings'.

Some commentators have translated it as 'coloured rooms', which, in my opinion, is incorrect. It is possible that rooms were painted from top to bottom depicting various things. Such rooms are commonly found in India even today, especially in the palaces and homes of Rajasthan. This form of wall painting is depicted in a picture of a *toranam* from Jaipur, in the next chapter about the palace of Lord Rama.

The opulent exteriors of the palace are mirrored inside by an opulent buffet of food around the clock as Valmiki states in Sanskrit: *vividhaiH annapaanaiH cha bhakshhaiH cha vividhaiH api*. *Anna and paana* mean 'cooked food and drinks'. Usually, *anna* means grains, such as rice and other cooked items. *Bhakshya,* according to the dictionaries, means 'fit to be eaten' or 'foods that require mastications or chewing'. *Bhakshya* is an interesting word that does not come under the meaning of *anna*. A meal of cooked food grains is called *bhojana* and, therefore, this word is always written separately when explaining the consumption of cooked food. A typical *bhojana* comprises a lavish assortment of cooked vegetables, food and grains, and almost always contains rice.

Bhojana does not include *bhakshaya* in Sanskrit literature, therefore, while reading *itihasa* or scriptures, one finds these words mentioned separately. Some translators have also mentioned *bhakshaya* as snacks, some as meat and some as roots because Indian snacks are usually crispy and need to be chewed and crushed properly, just as meat, roots and root vegetables. When the eating of meat and roots is specified in Sanskrit, it is written with *bhakshya* as a suffix. It is also used to describe the act of eating crudely due to hunger. This word usually implies eating in a crude manner as opposed to *bhojana*, which is eaten with sophistication.

The following are two images of typical Indian food. The first image is by Robert Sharp of Indian sweets, specifically prepared during Diwali. The second image is of a typical Indian buffet laid out with spices. These images were also included in my talk on *Amazing Ayodhya* hosted by Sangam Talks, held online on 25 April 2020 during the Coronavirus pandemic.

विविधैः अन्नपानैः च भक्ष्यैः

In a palace, one can expect a much larger and a more beautiful buffet laid out for an emperor. One can only imagine the aroma of the spicy curries, food and sweets wafting through the air of the palace as Maharaja Dasharatha walks in.

Along with delicious food, if Sage Valmiki mentions items to drink around the clock, it is likely that there was a bar at the palace. The following image is an illustration of possible drinks laid out in a bar in Treta Yuga. In India today, a large number of non-alcoholic drinks are consumed daily, such as coconut water, *neembu paani*, *aam panna*, *shikanji*, *chaach*, juices and squashes. These are consumed for beating the Indian summer heat as well as for their nutritious properties.

And because of all these things—trees, creepers, flowers, food and various decorative items, gold, silver and ivory pavilions and furniture, pools and flower- and fruit-bearing trees—Dasharatha's palace was shining and resembling heaven.

Sage Valmiki also mentions various birds residing in the palace. These birds will be described in detail in Part VI. For now, we will explore Lord Rama's palace.

Prince Rama's Palace

Prince Rama's palace, just like Emperor Dasharatha and Empress Kaikeyi's, was also magnificent. Here, Valmiki distinguishes between the two palaces by mentioning many differences. There are more animals as pets reared by Lord Rama and Devi Sita and their palace is grander. The description of the palace is mentioned when Sumantra, Dasharatha's charioteer, enters Lord Rama's palace where he was cohabiting with Devi Sita.

At first, just before entering, when Sumantra sees the palace of Prince Rama and Devi Sita, he observes that 'the palace was splendid, shining like the top of the Kailaasha mountain and radiant like Indra's palace'.

ततो ददर्श रुचिरं कैलासशिखरप्रभम् || २-१५-३१
रामवेश्म सुमन्तस्तु शक्रवेश्मसमप्रभम् |

tataH dadarshha ruchiram kailaasa sikharaprabham
|| 2-15-31
raamaveshma sumantraH tu shakra veshma
samaprabham |

The top of the mountain mentioned here is the peak of Kailaasha in the Himalayas. Kailaasha is the abode of Lord Shiva. Sage Valmiki further describes the palace in minute detail in the following *shlokas* from the *Ayodhya Kanda, sarga* 15.

Sumantra, upon entering the chambers, observes the following: 'Rama's palace was beautiful with large doors and adorned with hundreds of raised quadrangular seats. There were festooned decorations over doorways with gems and corals. It was adorned with various precious stones and the best of garlands. Pearls were scattered all over abundantly. It was decorated with sandal and aloe woods, spreading out beautiful smells like the peak of a Darddura Mountain. Sarus cranes and peacocks were singing sweetly. Figures of wolves and other art forms were sculptured here and there. It was attracting the eyes and minds of living beings by its brilliance. It was shining like a constellation of the moon and the sun. It was full of various kinds of birds. It was as high as the Meru mountain. Sumantra saw such a palace of Rama. People who came from different rural parts to see Rama's coronation were waiting with different gifts in their hands. That house, decorated with various diamonds, was looking high like a great cloud. Hunchbacked servants and servants of the Kirata tribe were moving all over the house.'

महाकवाटपिहितं वितर्दिशतशोभितम् || २-१५-३२
काञ्चनप्रतिमैकाग्रं मणिविद्रुमतोरणम् |
शारदाभ्रघनप्रख्यं दीप्तं मेरुगुहोपमम् || २-१५-३३
मणिभिर्वरमाल्यानां सुमहद्भिरलंकृतम् |
मुक्तामणिभिराकीर्णं चन्धनागुरुभूषितम् || २-१५-३४
गन्धान्मनोज्ञान् विसृजद्धार्दुरं शिखरं यथा |
सारसैश्च मयूरैश्च विनदद्भिर्विराजितम् || २-१५-३५
सुकृतेहामृगाकीर्णं सुकीर्णं भक्तिभिस्तथा |
मन्श्रक्षुश्च भूतानामाददत्तिग्मतेजसा || २-१५-३६
चन्द्रभास्करसंकाशम् कुबेरभवनोपमम् |
महेन्द्रधामप्रतिमं नानापक्षिसमाकुलम् || २-१५-३७
मेरुशृङ्गसमम् सूतो रामवेश्म ददर्श ह |
उपस्थितैः समाकीर्णम् जनैरञ्जलिकारिभिः || २-१५-३८
उपादाय समाक्रान्तैस्तथा जानपदैर्जनैः |
रामाभिषेकसुमुखैरुन्मुखैः समलम्कृतम् || २-१५-३९
महामेघसमप्रख्यमुद्ग्रं सुविभूषितम् |
नानारत्नसमाकीर्णं कुब्जकैरातकावृतम् || २-१५-४०

mahaakavaata pihitam vitardhishata shobhitam ||

2-15-32

kaaN^chana pratimaikaagram maNividruma toranam |

sharadaabhraghanaprakhyam diiptam

meruguhopamam || 2-15-33

maNibhiH varamaalyaanaam sumadbhiH
alankR^itam |
muktaamaNibhiH aakiirNam
chandanaagurubhuushhitam || 2-15-34
gandhaan manojJNaan visR^ijat daduram shikharam
yathaa I
saarasaiH mayuuraishcha vinadadbhiH viraajitam
|| 2-15-35
sukR^itehaa mR^igaakiirNam sukiirNam bhaktibhiH
tatha |
manaH chakshhushcha bhuutaanaam aadadat
tigmatejasaa || 2-15-36
chandrabhaaskaraa sankaasham kubera
bhavanopamana |
mahendra chaama pratimam
nanaapakshhisamaakulam || 2-15-37
merushR^ingasamam suutaH raamaveshma
dadarshaH |
upasthitaiH samaakiirNam janaiH aN^jalikaaribhiH
|| 2-15-38
upadaaya samaakrantaiH tathaa jaanapadaiH janiH |
raamaabhishheka sumukhaiH unmkhaiH
samalankR^itam || 2-15-39
mahaameghasamaprakhyam udagram
suvibhuushhitam |
naanaaratnasamaakiirNam kubja
kairaatakaavR^itam || 2-15-40

This picture of the Grand Palace of Bangkok, Thailand, has been shared to give readers a glimpse of how Lord Rama's palace might have looked like. In this image, Garuda, the *savaari* or vehicle mount of Lord Vishnu, is seen guarding the walls of the palace. Even though, the palace walls are painted in gold colour and embedded with coloured stones instead of real gold walls with diamonds, it still enthralls and dazzles the eyes and minds of visitors.

In the following *shloka*, from the same *sarga* as above, Valmiki makes another statement to capture the glory of Prince Rama's abode. He states, 'Then, Sumantra entered Rama's palace, which was like the top of a mountain, like an unmoving cloud, which contained houses equal to excellent *vimaanas* (divine cars), like crocodiles entering the ocean containing a number of precious stones. Nobody obstructed him.'

ततोऽद्रिकूटाचलमेघसन्निभं |
महाविमानोपमवेशमसंयुतम् |
अवार्यमाणः प्रविवेश सारथिः |
प्रभूतरत्नं मकरो यथार्णवम् || २-१५-४९

tataH adrikuutaachala magha sannibham |
mahaavimaanopama veshma samyutam |
avaaryamaaNaH pravivesha saarathiH |
prabhuutaratnam makaro yathaa arNavam || 2-15-49

The Sanskrit term *mahaavimaanopama veshma samyutam* translates to 'containing houses equal to excellent *vimaanas* (divine cars)'. Therefore, it is possible that there were more houses shaped like pyramids in the palace grounds. Some translators have commented it implies that the abode of Rama was a lofty or massive pyramidal-shaped building. Going by Valmiki's standard poetic jugglery, it is likely that both descriptions apply to the palace of Shri Rama.

While one can get a good description of the palace from the *shloka* mentioned above, a clear picture does not emerge in the mind of the readers of Kali Yuga, as many things have changed from Treta Yuga. For an enhanced mental picture of the palace, specific Sanskrit terms have been described in detail with the help of images. These descriptions have been divided into two parts, namely the arches and doorways and the gem-studded palace. These are described in detail in the following sections.

The Arches and Doorways

The Sanskrit term *maNividruma toranam* has been translated by a few experts as 'with festooned decorations over doorways with gems and corals'. A *toranam* is often confused with a chain or garland of flowers, leaves or ribbons, hung in a curve as a decoration. In India today, most *toranams* have been reduced to these kinds of hangings, but in *Vastu Shastra* they are very different.

The term *toranam* here means 'an arch that is beautifully designed and decorated'. This has been correctly stated by some commentators. It is being mentioned here so that the readers do not confuse between two different versions. According to the book *A Dictionary of Hindu Architecture* by Prassana Kumar Acharya (published by Oxford University Press in 1933), *toranam* means an arch. Therefore the *toranam* in the *shloka* is an arch too because Valmiki also describes these arches located at various entry points of Ayodhya district. These arches were also decorated with flowers and other auspicious things. This seems to be the case with Lord Rama and Devi Sita's palace too.

The following image is an example of a *toranam* from the book *Architecture of Manasara*. The image is used for illustrative purposes and gives us an idea of the *toranam* used in ancient times. The *toranam* shown below is the *kumbha toranam* or the 'water pot arch' or an 'Indian ewer arch'. According to the author, these *toranams* are mentioned in the Ramayana.

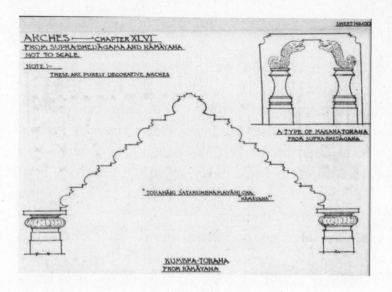

Next is an image of an intricately and aesthetically painted *toranam* from Patrika Gate, Jaipur, by Pijarn Jangsawang. Here, too, one can see the motifs of flowers and other beautiful shapes. Empress Kaikeyi's palace had similar painted walls. On the other hand, in Lord Rama's palace, these designs, instead of being painted, were embedded with various precious and semi-precious stones. This difference is visible owing to the different décor styles preferred by individual members of the royal family.

In the *shloka*, Sumantra beheld Rama's palace that was closed with (two) heavy panelled doors. A beautiful image of heavy panelled doors is also in The *Architecture of Manasara*. It has been shared here for illustrative purposes.

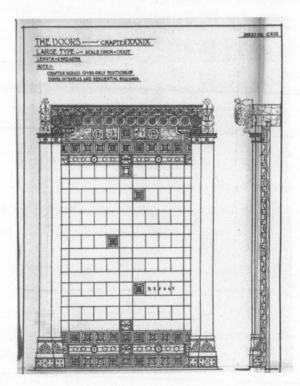

This variety of heavily panelled doors is still used in homes in many parts of India. They were used for both entrances to homes as well as forts or districts. An example of such a door is shown below. It was captured by user ctempoli and was edited further. Just as in the illustration above from the book, The *Architecture of Manasara*, the image below also features numerous square panels across the facade of the door. This image was also a part of the talk on *Amazing Ayodhya* on 25 April 2020.

Heavily Panelled Doors

Now that we have an idea of the arches and doorways present in the palace, can you guess the variety of gems that adorned the gold pannelled walls of Lord Rama and Devi Sita's palace?

The Gems of the Palace

Valmiki describes the palace of Rama as 'being studded with precious gems' over and over again in the Ramayana. This is perhaps done to emphasise the wealth of Lord Rama and the exquisiteness of his palace. While Kaikeyi's palace shines like the moon, Lord Rama's palace shines both like the sun and moon.

In all the descriptions of Lord Rama's palace in *shlokas* spread throughout the Ramayana, Valmiki never forgets to mention that it was completely embellished in jewels. In a later *shloka* from *Yuddha Kanda* of Valmiki Ramayana, there is another brief description of Lord Rama's palace This description is made when Lord Rama's *raja abhishekam* (coronation ceremony) is about to take place. In the *shloka* from the last *sarga*, Lord Rama says to Bharata, 'Give this great palace of mine which looks excellent with Ashoka gardens and consisting of pearls and cat's eye-gems to Sugreeva for his stay.' The *shloka* is mentioned below.

तच्च मद्भवनन् श्रेष्ठं साशोकवनिकं महत् ॥ ६-१२८-४५
मुक्तावैदूर्यसङ्कीर्णन् सुग्रीवस्य निवेदय ।

tat cha madbhavanam shreShTham saashokavanikam mahat || 6-128-45
muktaavaiduurya samkiirNam sugriivasya nivedaya |

All the *shlokas* discussed in this chapter name many gems. Some of those gems are: *muktaa (pearls)*, *vaiduurya* (chrysoberyl cat's eye), *vidruma* (coral), *maNi* (diamonds, and other precious gems). There must have been other gems too, but each one of them is not described in detail. Somehow, those gems that are important to Hindus and those used in astrology are mentioned specifically and repeatedly, like the pearl.

Since Lord Rama was born under the *Karaka Rashi* or 'moon sign of Cancer', that automatically makes the pearl his birthstone. One can suppose that is the reason why Valmiki keeps repeating that Lord Rama's palace is strewn with pearls. This is only a supposition and not necessarily the true reason, which is lost to time. However, this aspect of decoration with gems is most likely attributed to the fifth principle of *Vastu Shastra* and derived from the *vimaanas* of gods, which used to be embellished by gems in a similar fashion.

Amongst the many jewels in the palace is the *maNi*. The word *maNi* in Sanskrit means 'a jewel, gem or precious stone' or 'anything which is the best of its kind'. It is usually referred to as a diamond because it is the best jewel. It can refer to rubies, too, but one has to look for other clues to determine it correctly. When used with the name of another gem like *muktaamaNibhiH* (pearl gems), it implies either the best and the most expensive pearls or both diamonds and pearls. Likewise, *maNividruma* translates to either the best quality of corals or both diamonds and corals.

Below are some images of the gems, their shapes and their prices. All these were included in my talk on the Valmiki Ramayana on 25 April 2020.

IGI Certified 3.72 ct Chrysoberyl Cat's... ₹157,500 GemPundit.com

4.03ct Chrysoberyl Cat's Eye... ₹16,500 GemPundit.com

IGI Certified 2.3 ct Alexandrite Cat's... ₹71,700 GemPundit.com

4.06 ct Chrysoberyl Cat's Eye... ₹201,000 GemPundit.com

IGI Certified 4.52 ct Chrysoberyl Cat's... ₹192,000 GemPundit.com

5.36 ct Chrysoberyl Cat's Eye... ₹206,500 GemPundit.com

Chrysoberyl Cat's Eye

Corals Come in Different Shapes and Colours (red, pink, yellow)

Various Coloured Pearls and Diamonds

These gems and jewels are just a few of the *naanaaratnasamaakiirNam* or 'many, many types of diamonds/gems embedded' in the palace of Lord Rama and Devi Sita.

It is difficult for a layman to imagine how a palace studded with gems would always be shining bright or glowing as described by Valmiki. But one could visualise that in earlier times for light, instead of using bulbs, people used oil lamps or sticks that would be placed in spaces carved out in the walls of the palaces. The flickering light from these lamps would then be reflected and refracted in the various gems and diamonds, making them sparkle in diverse colours and shapes. Hence, the golden gem-studded walls of the palace would be shining during the day and illuminated and glowing at night.

The art of embedding raw uncut diamonds, pearls, corals and other precious and semi-precious gems in gold is still prevelant in India. Typically, raw uncut diamonds in gold can be seen in *polki* jewellery. *Polki* is very popular with Hindu women even today and often makes for heirloom pieces. An image of *polki* jewellery consisting of earrings and a neckpiece called *hasli* (sickle-shaped necklace) is given below, so that the reader can get an idea of how a diamond studded wall in the palace of Lord Rama and Devi Sita might have looked like.

By now, we have covered various interesting architectural details of the insides of Ayodhya. Another intriguing detail of Ayodhya is the *shataghnii*, which forms a defensive barrier for the fortress of Ayodhya. The next part of this book is devoted to solving the mystery of the *shataghnii*.

Part V

WEAPONS IN AYODHYA: THE MYSTERIOUS *SHATAGHNII*

Amongst the nine avatars of Vishnu that have walked the earth, the last three are called Rama. According to some beliefs, it is Balarama and not Gautama Buddha who is the ninth avatar of Vishnu. However, in certain regions, the image of Gautama Buddha remains but that of Krishna does not.

Below is an image displaying the 10 avatars of Lord Vishnu starting with the first avatar on the left. Each is shown by the weapons they possess or have mastered. The picture below is from Andhra Pradesh, India, and was made in the 19th century.

Lord Rama was trained in all kinds of weapons, but specifically in the use of the *baaNa* or bow. The name of the sixth avatar of Vishnu, Lord Parshurama, is a *samas* (compound word), which means Rama with an axe. *Parshu* in Sanskrit means an axe, which translates to *pharsaa* or *farsaa* in Hindi, a special kind of an axe. Balarama, the ninth avatar, is shown with a *hal* or a plough.

The distinction between the three Rama avatars is made by adding the names of their personal weapons or attributes to their formal given names, thereby making the sixth avatar as *Parshu*-Rama, the seventh avatar as *BaaNa*-Rama and the eight and ninth as *Bala*-Rama.

Because the images of individual avatars in the *Dasavatara* image shared previously could be indecipherable, a larger and clearer image of Parshurama is shown above. This image is also from Wikipedia and added by an Indonesian whose name I was unable to read. In this image, Lord Parshurama can be seen with his unique axe. The inscription in the previous image from Andhra Pradesh categorically says: *Parasurama Awataram: Rama with the Axe (Parasurama avatara)* then takes his stand, fells (cuts) the thick forests, clears the land.

The next image is a pen and ink drawing depicting Parasurama and Balarama, from an 'album of 51 drawings of buildings, sculpture and paintings in the temple and choultry of *Tirumala Nayyak* at Madurai, c.1801–05'. These drawings are from a carving that can be found in the Minakshi Sundareshvara Temple of Madurai and are done by an anonymous artist working in the Madurai (South Indian) style. In this picture too, both Balarama and Parshurama are shown with their weapons.

Parasurama Awataram: The Sixth Incarnation of Vishnu

Balarama Awataram: The Eighth Incarnation of Vishnu

In the *Dasavatara* painting from Andhra Pradesh, the description for Balrama says: *Balarama Awataram: Rama with the Plough* turns up the soil and teaches man to toil for food. In the Madurai drawing, a plough can be seen with Balrama and the specialised axe with Parshurama.

The description of Lord Rama in the Andhra Pradesh *Dasavatara* painting says: *Shree Rama Awataram: Rama with the Bow* against tyrants fights and thus defends the people's rights.

To elaborate this further, you can find below another painting of Rama made in the year 1816. He is depicted as a blue-skinned man and carrying a strung bow with a quiver full of arrows on his back and a single arrow in his right hand. The painting is made in the South Indian style and is currently displayed in the online collection of the British Museum.

As we can see, every avatar is either shown with his favourite weapon or the one he is most skilled at.

Weapons are used to describe these avatars in order to carve a distinct identity, so that the common man is able to distinguish between the avatars with imagery itself.

Likewise, both Ayodhya and Lanka have been clearly described by the kind of weaponry displayed to protect them from enemy attacks in the Ramayana.

A detailed description of the armoury is not given; rather only the visible weapons of protection are mentioned. Just like with the avatars, there is a distinct difference in the visible protective weaponry of the two cities. In the next chapter, we will discuss what kind of weaponry was visible on the ramparts of Ayodhya.

19

What Kind of Weaponry Was Visible in Ayodhya?

In one of the descriptive *shlokas* about the weapons kept in Ayodhya is a mention of the weapon *shataghnii*. This weapon 'describes' Ayodhya just as a *pharsaa* describes Parshurama. *Shataghnii* is an interesting weapon that is mentioned repeatedly in various ancient Hindu texts. What makes the *shataghnii* intriguing is that in every text that it is mentioned, its description varies. The changing description not only makes it mysterious but also difficult to understand.

One can assume that this weapon evolved through the times and was used in different forms. But what is consistent throughout its evolution is the description that it was 'thorny' or 'spiked'. For this book, as many valid references of *shataghnii* as possible have been taken in order to arrive at conclusions about what it really was. These references are mentioned with their sources and descriptions.

Valmiki says that Ayodhya had thousands of *shataghniis*. We can find this description in the first part of the Ramayana, the *Bala Kanda*. The corresponding *shloka* is mentioned below. In English, this *shloka* will be translated as, 'She, that prosperous city Ayodhya is muchly crammed with many a eulogist and panegyrist, yet she is highly

splendorous with many a bastion/watchtowers, flag
and hundreds of batteries of canons, and Dasharatha
dwells therein.'

सूत मागध संबाधाम् श्रीमतीम् अतुल प्रभाम् |
उच्चाट्टाल ध्वजवतीम् शतघ्नी शत संकुलाम् || १-५-११

*suuta maagadha sambaadhaam shriimatiim atula
prabhaam |
ucchaaTTaala dhvajavatiim shataghnii shata
samkulaam || 1-5-11*

Valmiki uses the word *shataghnii* in the same line of
the *shloka* to define the watchtowers of Ayodhya—
ucchaaTTaala dhvajavatiim shataghnii shata samkulaam.
One of the conclusions we can draw is that the weapon
stood out just like watchtowers with hoisted flags did
on a city fort or rampart. It is possible this weapon
was placed all along the ramparts. Perhaps, it is with
the *aTTaala* mentioned in the *shloka* above. Or was it
in the *aTTaala* itself? This is a mystery to be solved.
In this translation of the Valmiki Ramayana by Shri
Desiraju Hanumanta Rao, hundreds of *shataghniis* are
mentioned as batteries of a cannon. But what sort of
cannon is spiky?

In order to unravel the mystery of the *shatghanii*,
it has to be first deciphered where it was placed and
what was in its vicinity. For this reason, we will first try
and decide what *aTTaalas* are. The *aTTaalas* of both
Ayodhya and Lanka will be decoded since this weapon
was found on both fortresses.

20

Decoding the *aTTaala*

The word for watchtowers in Sanskrit is *aTTaalaka* or *aTTala*. *ATTa* and *aTTala* both mean 'high and lofty' and *alaka* in Sanskrit means curls or locks. *ATTalaka* has various meanings, such as observatories, watchtowers and towers. It is also probable that these watchtowers were circular or curled in shape, just like the locks of a young girl, hence the name. Most watchtowers of ancient India used to be circular and almost all of them were observatories. Valmiki also stated that from each of these lofty bastions and watchtowers, the flag of Kosala Empire flew high.

Other meanings for *aTTaalaka* are an apartment on the roof, an upper storey and a palace. Perhaps because of this, *aTTaalaka* has been wrongly translated to mansions in various versions of the Ramayana. Mansions in the Ramayana are called *vimaanas,* which means a multistoreyed building with a pyramidal shape. Valmiki clearly states that the *aTTaalaka*-s of Ayodhya were tall or high. What Valmiki means is that they were taller than the ramparts. This kind of design is still common in Indian forts.

The following image is of the Gwalior Fort, Madhya Pradesh. You can clearly see the circular watchtowers here. All these watchtowers are connected with a rampart. A rampart is a defensive or protective barrier, especially a protective wall around a castle or city or stronghold made of stone with a broad top that serves as a walkway.

Another image of the Gwalior Fort that gives us more clarity about the *aTTaalaka* is one captured by Udit Sharma and uploaded on Wikipedia. Observe the varied numbers of watchtowers and bastions that are scattered all around the fortress, and their circular shapes.

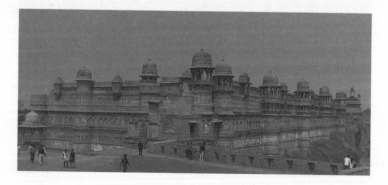

The small projecting part of a fortification, especially if it is built at an angle to the line of a wall, is called a bastion. Such bastions were placed on the four corners of the fort. Because of its 90-degree placement, a bastion allows for defensive fire in several directions. These angular bastions were more common in the West than in our country. In India, the bastion is in the same line as the walls of the fortress. Instead, it is the towers that project at an angle on the rampart/boundary wall of the fortress. A point is being made to differentiate between a bastion and a watchtower, as some translators have said that *aTTaalaka* means 'bastion' or a 'mansion'.

Below is another example of an *aTTaalaka* of the Jaigarh Fort, Rajasthan. This is not perfectly circular in its structure at the base but has a perfectly circular walkway around it (towards the top from the middle).

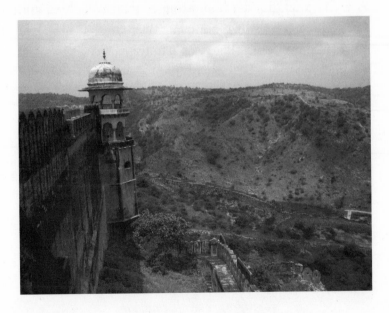

These watchtowers were an integral part of the design and construction of forts, along with many *shataghniis*. These are a part of *Vastu Shastra* and are mentioned in books that deal with the construction of *durgas*. *Durga* in Sanskrit means 'impenetrable'. In the case of forts, it implies an impenetrable, unassailable stronghold. The name of the revered Hindu Goddess Durgaa is derived from the same root in Sanskrit. The name Durgaa also means inaccessible or invincible.

For Lanka, too, Valmiki describes the city possessing many *shatghaniis*. This can be found in *sarga* 5 of the *Sundar Kanda* where Hanumana describes the city of Lanka. He says that there are so many *shatghaniis* and *shoolas* that they look like a maiden's hair, and the *aTTaalakas* look like the *avatamsa* of a maiden. The various *shataghniis* and *shoolas* are falling over the maidens' *avantamsa*. One has to remember that Lanka as a city was grander and stronger than Ayodhya, and situated on top of a mountain. Therefore, it also had more fortifications. The English translation given is: 'Hanumana saw the city of Lanka with buttress and enclosure wall as her hip and loins, the vast body of water in the moat as her raiment, *shataghniis* and *shoolas* as her locks, the mansions as her earrings, constructed by thought. He reached the northern gate and thought thus.'

पप्रप्राकारजघनां विपुलाम्बुनवाम्बराम् |
शतघ्रीशूलकेशान्तामट्टालकवतंसकाम् || ५-२-२१
मन्सेव कृतां लङ्कां निर्मितां विश्वकर्मणा |
द्वारमुत्तरमासाद्य चिन्तयामास वानरः || ५-२-२२

vaprapraakaara jaghanaam
vipulaambunavaambaraam |
shataghnii shuula keshantaam
aTTaalakavataMsakaam || 5-2-21

manas eva kR^ita laN^kaam nirmitaam
vishvakarmaNaa |
dvaaram uttaram aasaadya chintayaamaasa
vaanaraH || 5-2-22

The English translation of this *shloka* is incomplete, as it misses out certain parts that are in Sanskrit. The correct translation implies that Hanumana is thinking to himself that Vishvakarama, who has constructed Lanka, did so while keeping in mind a beautiful lady. The buttress and enclosure wall of the fortress look like her hips and loins with the vast body of moat water as her raiment. *Shataghniis* and *shoolas* as her locks, the watchtowers as her diadem, and thus while thinking, he reached the northern gate.

Valmiki uses the word *aTTaalakavataMsakaam* to describe the watchtowers of Lanka. Along with *aTTaalaka*, he mentions *avatamsa*. The word *avatamsa*, spelled as *ava-tamsa* or *ava-tamsaka* in Sanskrit dictionaries, has been translated to a wreath, a diadem, a ring-shaped ornament, and even earrings in certain places. In earlier yugas, both sexes would wear ornaments, including earrings and diadems.

In Hindu history, there aren't many suggestions of women wearing wreaths except for those living in jungles. It was more Greek in nature than Hindu, though diadems and ring-shaped ornaments were popular in Bharat. Following is an example of a typical Indian diadem made up of gold, inset with a garnet. This diadem is from the state of Jammu and Kashmir from the 9th or 10th century, and is part of the collection at The Metropolitan Museum of Art in

New York. It looks similar to a *mathapatti* worn by Hindu women even today. Brides usually wear one on the forehead during wedding.

Hindu brides today, like in the image below by Gajendra Bhati, wear a similar *avatamsa* or *mathapatti*.

Of course, with time, small alterations have happened to the shape. But, if we go back in the past, we find the exact shape that is being spoken about in the Ramayana. Here is a picture of an Egyptian gold diadem, which served as the crown of Princess Sit-Hathor Yunet, the daughter of the 12th-dynasty pharaoh, Senusret II. If we go further back in time, we find similar slender rectangular band-like diadems used by the ancient Greeks too. The image below is by Hans Ollermann on Wikipedia.

It is very likely that the watchtowers of Lanka were shaped like a slender rectangular band on which various *shataghniis* and *shoolas* were falling over.

These images are shared so that a reader does not confuse a diadem with a tiara. A tiara is higher in the middle and tapers down at the back, while a diadem goes all the way around the head. It is important to note these little distinctions to understand the exact construction of the fortress. A tiara-shaped fortification would be weaker on the sides which are lower.

The following is a Bavarian Lover's Knot Tiara
captured by José Luiz Bernardes Ribeiro and found on
Wikipedia. It shows the typical tapering down towards
the back. This was not the shape that is mentioned to
describe Lanka in the Ramayana.

In previous yugas, it is likely that an *avatamsa* was worn
by all women, especially women of rank. Diadems
were worn by women for decorative purposes as well
as to suggest rank. They could be worn at all times; no
special occasion was required. This kind of jewellery
was common all over the world. Apart from ancient
Hindus, ancient Egyptians and the Greeks too, going
back as far as the 3rd-century BC, wore diadems.

In earlier times, Hindu women from good or noble
families were never seen with open hair. It was considered
immoral, disrespectful and crude, especially when in
public. Their hair was always washed, dried, oiled and
tied up under their diadems, tiaras, crowns or other
hair ornaments. This is why in the epic Mahabharata,
Queen Draupadi refuses to tie her hair unless her five
husbands avenge the assault on her dignity by killing

the aggressors. Even Kautilya pledged to not tie his *shikha* until he avenged his dishonour by overthrowing Emperor Dhana Nanda of the Nanda dynasty. *Shikha* is a tuft of hair on either the left side or on top of the head which is never shaved or cut. Usually Brahmins adorn a *shikha*, kept twisted in a knot. In Sanskrit, *shikha* means a peak or a crest.

In the image below of Lord Shiva, a clear picture of an *avatamsa* can be seen on his forehead. This image of a bronze sculpture of Lord Shiva is from the Chola Period, India, and is taken by Mike Steele and uploaded on Flikr.

Even using various images of diadems to explain what Valmiki talks about cannot create a mental image of the Lankan fortress, unless an example of a fortress is given alongside. Therefore, shared next is an interesting example of diadem-shaped watchtowers, as seen on the Derawar Fortress in West Punjab, Pakistan. The Indian state of Punjab was divided and the western portion became a part of Pakistan after the Partition of India in 1947. Derawar Fortress was originally named Dera

Rawal and was built in the 9th century AD by Rai Jajja Bhatti, a Hindu ruler of the Bhatti clan from Jaisalmer, Rajasthan, India. The image has been sourced from Wikipedia and captured by user Fassifarrooq.

In the image, notice that the watchtowers are as tall as the ramparts. They have a circular design, but they are all of even height. This is exactly what Valmiki was trying to say with the word *avatamsa to* describe the watchtowers. The fortress of Lanka was shaped in this manner, and on the ramparts of such a fortress numerous *shataghnii*s and *shoola*s were placed, which made it look like a maiden's hair was falling over her diadem. The style of the Derawar Fortress is same as that of the fortress in Lanka, erected on a mountain. That is why Valmiki accurately describes it as *aTTaalakavataMsakaam*.

Both the *aTTaalakas* of Lanka and Ayodhya had similar weaponry placed on them. While both had *shataghniis*, Ayodha did not have *shoolas* on its ramparts. This is a prominent difference stated by Valmiki.

Now that the *aTTaalakas* of Ayodhya and Lanka and their different styles and shapes are decoded, let's try and decipher the mysterious *shataghnii, placed on these aTTaalakas*. In order to understand this mysterious weapon, in the next chapter we will go through many sources and try to come up with an image of this weapon. Apart from the Ramayana, an important source for describing the *shataghniis* are the Vedas. Various commentators have also given their opinion on the weapon. Those descriptions that did not make sense or belonged to another category of weapons but wrongly claimed as *shataghnii* have been excluded as sources in this book.

Decoding the Mysterious
shataghnii

One of the most important descriptions of the *shataghnii* is mentioned in the *Dhanurveda* written by Rishi Vashishtha. *Dhanurveda* is a part of the Vedas and a legitimate source because they were written before the time of Lord Rama. It is also pertinent to mention that Vashishtha was one of the teachers of Lord Rama. He was the family priest and guru of Raghu Kula or the Raghu Dynasty to which Lord Rama belongs. He is also supposed to be the guru of Ikshvaku, the son of Manu from whom the Solar Race starts. Rishi Vashishtha is one of the *sapt rishis* of the current *manavantara* who survived the *pralaya* and is still considered to be alive.

The following *shloka* is mentioned in the *Dhanurveda* about *shataghniis*. The *shloka* translates to, 'The intelligent should, for the protection of the throne, establish *shataghniis* on the stronghold. With the *shataghniis*, flammables should be kept in adequate quantities.'

सिंहासनस्य रक्षार्थं शतघ्नं स्थापयेत् गढे ।
रंजकंबहुलं तत्र स्थाप्यं वटयो धीमता ? ॥७५॥

siMhAsanasya rakShArthaM shataghnaM
sthApayet gaDhe |
raMjakaMbahulaM tatra sthApyaM vaTayo
dhImatA ? ||75||

In the various translations and commentaries of the
Valmiki Ramayana, most English commentators have
skipped giving an exact explanation of this weapon.
On the other hand, the Sanskrit commentators express
that *shataghnii* was 'a special kind of weapon that was
kept on the rampart'. They all agree that 'it killed many
men'. Their comments on this mysterious weapon are
mentioned below.

Amruta Kataka
शतं पुरुषान् हन्तीति शतघ्नीअयोभारनिर्मितः प्राकारोपरि
स्थापितो मुसलविशेषः । 'अमनुष्यकर्तृके च' इति हन्तेष्टक् ।
उपधालोपादि ।।

Govindaraja
शतघ्नी प्राकारस्थयन्त्रविशेषः। "शतघ्नी तु चतुस्ताला
लोहकण्टकसञ्चिता" इति यादवः। शतशब्दोऽनन्तवचनः। "शतं
सहस्रमयुतं सर्वमानन्त्यवाचकम्" इत्युक्तेः।
अनेकशतघ्नीसंवृताम् ।।

Nagesa Bhatta
शतघ्यो नाम प्राकारसंरक्षणार्थमयोभारनिर्मिताः
प्राकारोपरिस्थापिता आयुधविशेषाः ।।

Amruta Kataka
shataM puruShAn hantIti
shataghnIayobhAranirmitaH prAkAropari sthApito
musalavisheShaH | 'amanuShyakartRRike cha' iti
hanteShTak | upadhAlopAdi

Govindaraja
shataghnI prAkArasthayantravisheShaH | "shataghnI
tu chatustAlA lohakaNTakasa~nchitA" iti yAdavaH
| shatashabdo.anantavachanaH | "shataM
sahasramayutaM sarvamAnantyavAchakam" ityukteH
| anekashataghnIsaMvRRitAm || 1-5-11 ||

Nagesa Bhatta
shataghnyo nAma
prAkArasaMrakShaNArthamayobhAranirmitAH
prAkAroparisthApitA AyudhavisheShAH

Commentator Amruta Kataka states, 'A *shataghnii* killed hundreds of men. It was constructed out of a massive block of metal (iron) which is huge and heavy. It is placed upon the ramparts of the fort. It is a special kind of *musala* or pestle.'

Some believe a *musala* to be a mace, but that is incorrect. Hindus today, too, use the *musala* to mash, hammer, batter or beat grains. The following is an image of a *musala* or pestle. A mace is called a *gadaa* in Sanskrit. The *musala* could be closer to a club but not a mace because the latter holds most of its weight on one end. On the contrary, the weight of a club is distributed more gradually, from the narrow end to the wider end. A club, therefore, could be similar to a pestle but not a mace.

The image given below is of a smaller version of an *okhali* and *musal* (mortar and pestle), which is found in every Indian kitchen. The average *okhali* and *musal* are much larger in shape and size.

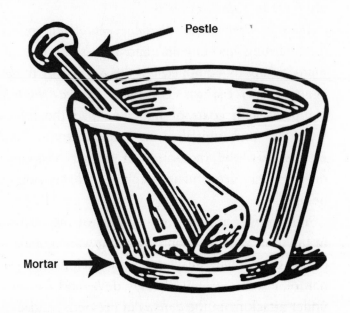

Commentator Govindaraja mentions that the *shataghnii* is *chatuH taalaa* (four *taalaa*) long and numerous iron thorns are embedded in it. It silences hundreds of promises of men, which means that with the men, it killed their words and promises as well. There are many *shataghniis* laid out (on the ramparts).

Commentator Nagesa Bhatta specifies that *shataghnii* is a special weapon made of metal and placed on the ramparts. It is huge and heavy, and used for the protection of the rampart (fort).

The commentary by Desiraju Hanumanta Rao (valmikiramayan.net) on *shataghnii* states, 'This *shataghnii* literally is that which can kill a thousand people, and it is said to be a cannon and also said to be thorny weapon: *shataghnii catuH talaa loha kaNTaka sa~ncitaa | ayaH kaNTaka sa~ncchannaa mahatii shilaa*. Elaborate accounts of this *shataghnii, kshipaNi* are there in *Yajur aaraNyaka*.'

In the *Brahmanda Purana*, *shataghnii* refers to 'bombarding instruments' and represents one of the many weapons equipped by the *daityas* in their war against Devi Lalitaa. 'Crores of *daityas* were fully equipped with coats of mail and had the following weapons and missiles in their hands (namely *shataghniis*), and thousands of similar weapons and missiles, very dreadful and capable of destroying living beings.'

The *daityas* are the step-siblings of the devas and, in the past, were constantly waging wars against them out of their innate mischevious, malicious and jealous nature. For this reason, all devis, devas and *devatas* were under attack from the *daityas* in previous yugas. Many people believe that both *devata* and *daitya* are human. But that isn't true. Since they are not the children of Manu, they cannot be categorised as human beings. Also, they are no longer on earth unlike in the past when some of them used to either reside or frequent planet earth.

When in war, the *daityas* were well prepared and donned coats of mail or chainmail armour suits. An image of coats of mail is given below for illustrative purposes. The image has been sourced from paramounthandicrafts.com.

Both Ayurveda and the *Garuda Purana* mention that '*shataghnii* is a thick, stick-like growth in the throat, studded over with fleshy papillae and attended with diverse kinds of pain'. This disease is attributed to the concerted action of the deranged *Vayu*, *Pitta* and *Kapha*, and invariably proves fatal.

Ayurveda and the *Garuda Purana* are synchronous with the rest of the commentaries that *shataghnii* is studded with papillae. The papillae are small, rounded protuberances on a part or organ of the body, like the tongue.

Next is a macro photo of a cat cleaning itself by Jennifer Leigh on Wikipedia. The image shows hooked papilla on the tongue. This image is just a visual cue to how papillae look on the tongue. The diseased human papillae tongue images were a little too gross to share.

From the time of *Dhanur Veda* to the time of Ramayana, the evolution of *shataghnii* continues. By the time Kali Yuga arrives, *shataghnii* metamorphosises from cannons to pillars. In the eighteenth chapter of the *Arthashastra*, the Superintendent of the Armoury, Kautilya talks of *shataghnii* as a moveable weapon. Kautilya classifies these in the same line as *chakra* (discus or war quoit), *gadaa* (mace), *trishul* (trident), etc. In the commentary on that chapter, it is specified that *shataghnii* is a big pillar with an immense number of sharp points on its surface and situated on the top of a fort wall.

According to chapter 23 of *Natya Shastra*, treatise on the ancient Hindu performing arts, the *shataghnii* refers to a weapon that should measure eight *taalaa*. A *taala* is a unit of measurement; its plural form is known as *taalaa*. A real-sized replica of this weapon was to be designed and used in dramatic plays by experts using proper measurements. It was carried by actors engaged in fights or angry conflicts.

The DDSA: Practical Sanskrit-English Dictionary described *shataghnii* as 'a kind of weapon used as a missile, supposed by some to be a sort of rocket, but described by others as a huge stone, studded with iron spikes and four *taalaa* in length.'

The descriptions of a rocket in the above dictionary are from the earlier yugas. By the time the Mahabharata Era came along, a huge stone studded with iron spikes started getting called a *shataghnii*. Considering that the Ramayanic Era predates the Mahabharata Era, this particular description will not be dwelt upon.

In certain places of the *Sundara Kanda* of the Valmiki Ramayana, the *shataghnii* has been explained by commentators as a *koota shaalmalii*, the weapon of Yamraja, also known as Yama. This is because in the Ramayana itself, when Hanumana goes to Lanka, he sees the *rakshasas* carrying *shataghnii* on them. The corresponding *shloka* is given below.

धन्विनः खड्गिनः चैव शतघ्री मुसल आयुधान् || ५-४-१७
परिघ उत्तम हस्तामः च विचित्र कवच उज्ज्वलान् |

dhanvinaH khaDginashcaiva
shataghnimusalaayudhaan || 5-4-17
parighottamahastaamshca vicitrakavacojjvalaan |

The translation in English for the *shloka* is, 'Those who carried bows and arrows, those who carried swords, those who carried pestles and clubs as weapons, those who carried excellent Parighas in their hands, those who shone with strange armour.'

In this *shloka*, the *shataghnii* is translated as a pestle and the *musala* as a club. Incidentally, both of them are often depicted as weapons of Yama. To explore these weapons, two old images of Yama are shared below.

The first image is sourced from The British Museum and was painted in 1850 by an unknown artist in Tamil Nadu, India. This is a gouache painting on paper from an album of 82 paintings of Hindu deities. The description along with it says, '*Yama*: Four-armed and dark-complexioned Yama rides on his bejewelled and caparisoned buffalo. In his upper right hand is the *danda* (staff). His upper left is in *suchi mudra*, his lower right is in *abhaya mudra*, and his lower left is by his waist.'

Yama

In this image, while the description says Yama carries a *danda* (staff), the *danda* actually looks like a pestle.

The next painting, again sourced from The British Museum, was painted in 1820 by an unknown artist. The description says that it is a painting of *Dikpala Yama*. He is depicted as blue-skinned, four-armed and seated on his *vahana*, the buffalo. In his two upper hands, he holds a mace (right) and lasso (left). His lower hands are held in *varada mudra* (left) and *abhaya mudra* (right). In front walks an attendant carrying a mace, while the attendant behind holds a parasol above the God.

Here, a mace or a club is depicted clearly. But in both, the images the correct image of *koota shaalmlii* is not depicted. Instead, the weapon he holds undergoes changes. Of late, he is depicted with just a stick in his hand.

In deciphering the etymology of the word *koota shaalmalii*, we get two words *koota* and *shaalmlii*. In Hindi, the action that is performed with the *musala* is called *kootna*. As mentioned earlier, according to the commentator Amruta Katak, *shataghnii* was supposed to be like the *musala*. But *koota* in Sanskrit also stands for different types of instruments and not only the pestle. *Koota* also means a ploughshare and a mallet. To decipher this instrument, two images of a ploughshare and one of a mallet are shared with their descriptions.

The image below is of a handheld ploughshare. In certain images of Yama, he is shown holding this weapon as well. This image, sourced from Wikipedia, is from the Czech Republic, uploaded by user Jitka Erbenová. This instrument of the field has remained constant in its design throughout Eurasia and is used in farms to this day.

The image below is taken from page 84 of *Bible Lands, Their Modern Customs and Manners Illustrative of Scripture* belonging to the British Library (source: Flickr). It shows the plough of the past. These kinds of ploughs are still used in rural India. The contraption labelled 2 is the ploughshare.

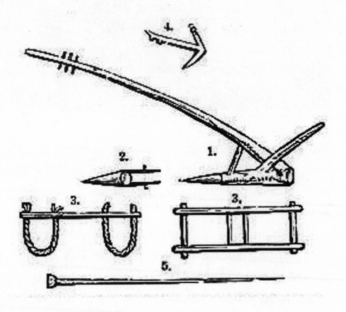

The next image is of a mallet used for hammering meat with thorns or spikes on them. Interestingly enough, judges in courts across the world use wooden mallets (without spikes). Yama, too, is a karmic judge of souls, the God of justice. He is the brother of Vaivasvata Manu, and he also has a twin sister, Yami (or Yamuna).

Now that various types of *kootas* have been explored, let's move to deciphering the *shaalmalii*. The Shalmali tree is rather common in the Indian subcontinent; its surface is full of thorns.

Older pictures of Yamraja have accurately depicted him holding a long weapon that has lots of thorns on it, just like the Shalmali tree. Unfortunately, this image is no longer in circulation, therefore, it could not be reproduced for this book.

In other paintings or sculptures of Yama, his weapon changes into a *gadaa*. In some places, it changes into a smooth stick or a club (as shown previously). These depictions are inaccurate, as the Sanskrit word *shaalmalii* is descriptive of an unusual tree. This tree is also called the Seemul tree or silk-cotton tree, Bombax Heptaphyllum or Salmalia Malabarica. It is a very tall and thorny tree with red flowers. Therefore, a *koota* made out of the wood of this tree would never have a smooth surface.

According to Hindu lore, the thorns of *shaalmalii* are used for torture in one of the hells, inspiring the name of that particular hell. There are numerous hells described in Hindu scriptures where sinners get punished according to their sins. These come under the guardianship of Lord Yama. Below is the image of a Ceiba Speciosa Barbed Tree captured by user Baba Mu (source: needpix). The barbed spikes on this tree are clearly visible. The Bombax Ceiba is a similar tree with many such spikes. One can now clearly visualise what a pestle made from this wood would look like.

While we are clear about what a *koota shaalmalii* looks like, after going through so many references of commentators combined with images, a hazy mental picture of a *shataghnii* forms. With numerous references, it becomes obvious that there are more than one or two varieties of *shataghniis*. Each variety has some differences in size, shape and use. But the common feature is the barbs or spikes. These barbs, spikes or thorns are either many in number (mallet) or just one (ploughshare), and they seem hazardous for anyone who come in contact with them. Perhaps, because of the barbs and thorns embedded in different types of weapons, they were called *shataghniis*.

If there is only one barb or thorn on the *shataghnii*, and it looks like the ploughshare, then it is purely a missile or a rocket that is used today. If it has many barbs or thorns on it like the mallet, then it is unusual because such a weapon is not found these days. In order to further decode this mystery, let's pay attention to information on their sizes.

1. According to *Natya Shastra*, a *shataghnii* should measure eight *tala*.

2. According to Desiraju Hanumanta Rao's commentary on valmikiramayan.net, which is similar to Govindraja's commentary in Sanskrit, the *shataghnii* is four *tala*. Rao further adds that it is a massive stone with iron/steel thorns on it. This description of the stone with iron spikes comes from the book, *Uvasagadasao*.

As mentioned earlier, *taalaa* is a measurement of size. One *taala*, according to Vaman Shivaram Apte's Sanskrit dictionary, is the length between the thumb and the middle finger when outstretched. But this measurement is not so simplistic and *taala* not only measures length but also the shape and proportion of the sculpture/weapon/object. According to Gopinath Rao, the canons of iconometry (*Vastu Shastra*) follow a complex system called *taalamana*. He explains further that the human face is equal to the length of one *taalaa* (or twelve *angulas*), the length from the throat to the navel is two *taalaa*, from navel to the top of the knee is three *taalaa*, and from the lower knee to the ankle is two *taalaa*, making the total height of a human equal to eight *taalaa*.

Dwarf figures are made following a *chatus taalaa* or a four-*taala* system where the total height is four times the face length. Canons of iconometry describe 10 divisions from the *eka taala* (single *tala*) to *dasa taalaa* (or 10 *taalaa*). The system makes use of the fact that persons with a disproportionately larger face length appear shorter and those with shorter faces appear taller. The faces of dwarves are considerably larger than the faces of taller humans, in comparison to their bodies.

Therefore, we have two lengths and sizes of the *shataghnii*: a regular eight *taalaa* length with the head being the smaller portion, and a dwarf length of four *taalaa* with the head being bigger.

Based on the information of *koota shaalmalii* and *chatus taalaa* length, two illustrations are drawn. Both these weapons are four *taalaa* long and are broader at the top. Their spikes are limited to the first *taalaa* of the weapon, otherwise it would not be possible to carry it on the shoulder.

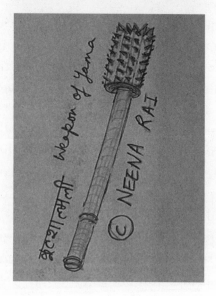

If the *shataghnii* was shaped like the *koota shaalmalii*,
then it is likely that it was like one of the weapons in the
hand-drawn images above. This would be the first type
of *shataghanii*, which could be used by hand (as seen
by Hanumana in Lanka). It is unlikely to be thrown at
the enemy, but it could be fired from a cannon. The first
illustration of the *koota shaalmalii* is more aerodynamic
(if fired) than the second. The second illustration,

when used in battle to wound the enemy, would be more formidable.

The second type of *shataghnii* is the missile, which is fired from some sort of cannon. It would not be carried in the hand or used in physical hand-to-hand combat. The length of this missile could be either four *taalaa* (short) or eight *taalaa* (long).

Today, missiles can both be long or short and can have spikes. Interestingly enough, there is an Israeli missile called Spike, which has a few spikes; it is an anti-tank guided missile (ATGM). An image of this missile, captured by Dave1185, Wikipedia, is shared below.

Any modern missile includes a Command Launch Unit (CLU) made up of a launch tube and its base. The launch tube houses the missile and the base supports the launch tube. The base could have wheels or a tripod (as shown above). The cannon (launch unit) of the Spike ATGM missile is smaller and more compact, unlike the cannon of the *shataghnii* (as explained in the commentaries of the Ramayana). As per the Ramayana, the launch unit of a *shataghnii* is large and heavy.

To explore larger launch units that fit the description of the commentaries, an image from the United States Marine Corps, on Wikipedia, featuring M198 155 mm Howitzers is shared. This image is shown for the reader to grasp the enormity of the weapon as described in the Ramayana. It is possible that this sort of a weapon was kept alongst the rampart of Ayodhya to fire *shataghniis*. A weapon like this would surely be visible from the rampart of both Ayodhya and Lanka. This sort of cannon could launch both the four and the eight *taalaa shataghniis*.

Based on the descriptions given above of the rocket/missile launchers, a sketch is made of the *shataghanii* that is four *taalaa* long with iron spikes all over. Its illustration is shared next. This missile could be easily moved around and fired from cannons. The non-thorny part of the *shataghanii* would be fitted in the launch tube.

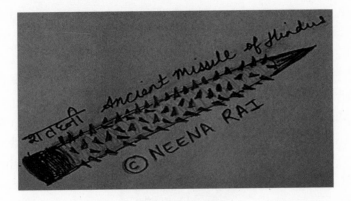

This weapon would be utterly lethal and true to its name *shataghnii*, which means killer of hundreds, if it fragmented after being fired. Fragmentation is the process by which the casing of a projectile missile is shattered by the detonation of its explosive filler. For any fragmentation to occur, pre-formed or embedded fragments should be present on the weapon. These fragments or splinters could be of various sizes and shapes, such as spheres, cubes, rods, or even *kaNtakas* (thorns). Ideally, the fragments or shrapnels of this lethal missile would be held rigidly within or on the body of the missle until the explosive filling is detonated.

A perfect example of fragmentation, after being detonated, is the hand grenade. The Second World War- era MK2 Grenade made by the Americans used to have grooves on the exterior. The following image by J.L. Dubois, Wikipedia, is of such a grenade that fragments after detonation. Once this grenade was detonated, the fragments would pierce, killing or maiming the enemy.

By now it's clear that the concept behind using fragments like *kaNtaka* (thorn) on the body of the missile was to cause as much damage as possible. Based on all the images and illustrations shared above, one could speculate that the cannon of the *shataghnii* would have a rather heavy base with a launch tube of eight *taalaa* and the missile (full of thorns) of four *taalaa*. Only in such a case can the different descriptions of various commentaries combine to make sense.

There must be other forms of *shataghniis* mentioned in other sources, but the one I have arrived at takes into consideration evidence from the Ramayanic Era and the ones preceding that. As mentioned earlier, this weapon has undergone changes from time to time and is open to various other interpretations, especially from post-Ramayanic Era sources.

Part VI

ANIMALS IN
AYODHYA

Every country today is teeming with cars, bikes, trains and buses for transport. Not only do these help citizens travel within the boundaries of cities but also help reach other states and countries. Before the invention of the petrol-powered internal combustion engine of the automobile in 1885, humans used vehicles drawn by horses, donkeys, bulls, elephants and camels.

Just like both currency (cash) and grains are considered wealth by Hindus, prosperity was denoted by the number of animals an individual or a kingdom possessed. In order to ascertain status, people today look at which luxury car one drives: a Jaguar, a Mercedes or a Porsche? In the olden days, the number of animals decided that. They were expensive to not only purchase, but also to maintain—just like the luxury cars of today.

In the Valmiki Ramayana, the prosperity of Ayodhya as a district and Kosala as a kingdom is revealed by the presence of various animals. Sage Valmiki pays particular attention to elephants and their breeding in the city. Elephants were the most important animals to own for a kingdom. It was not only the vehicle of choice for the king, but elepehants also helped win wars. Ancient Hindu kings valued the elephant in war so much that some believed that 'an army without elephants is as despicable as a forest without a lion, a kingdom without a king or valour unaided by weapons'. This quote is found in the Sanskrit book *Sharngadhara-paddhati* (Sharngadhara's Guidebook) and is also referenced in P.C. Chakarvarti's *The Art of War in Ancient India*.

Along with elephants, horses, too, were the preferred vehicle of warriors and kings alike. Elephants and horses were both recognised as a part of royal and military possessions. In wars, kings preferred to ride chariots led by horses, perhaps because they were very fast. The elephants were the preferred vehicles of the elite, both in war and otherwise.

In Hindu history, there are enough references to kings and other noblemen riding on the back of elephants to tour their territory. In the book *The Architecture of Manasara*, designs of palaces included specific areas that were allotted to keep elephants. In Hindi, such places are called *hathkhana* or even *haudas or hawdas*. A h*auda or hawda* is also the term used to denote an uncovered box or chair on an elephant upon which or in which the rider sits. Elephants were kept as pet animals even in post-independent India.

Sage Valmiki writes that Lord Rama was a champion elephant and horse rider, and excelled in tactical charioting too. This is mentioned in the *Bala Kanda*, *sarga* 18, of the Ramayana.

गज स्कन्धे अश्व पृष्ठे च रथ चर्यासु सम्मतः || १-१८-२७
धनुर्वेदे च निरतः पितुः शुश्रूषणे रतः |

gaja skandhe; ashva pR^iST te cha ratha charyaasu
sammataH || 1-18-27
dhanuH vede cha nirataH pituH shushruushaNe rataH |

The above *shloka* implies, 'Rama is admittedly a champion of riding elephants and horses, also in tactical charioting, and he rejoices in the art of archery, and absorbed in the obedient service of his father.' It is relevant to mention here that no man can be a tactical charioteer unless he is adept at handling horses.

A description of the chariot of Lord Rama is made in the *Ayodhya Kanda*, *sarga* 15, when he is getting ready to be crowned King. The *shloka* is mentioned below and translates to, 'Golden jars filled with water, the well-decorated throne and a chariot spread well with bright and shiny tigerskin (were kept ready).'

काञ्चना जलकुमाभश्च भद्रपीठं स्वलङ्तम् || २-१५-४
रथश्च सम्यगा स्तीर्णोभास्वता व्याग्रचर्मणा |

kaaJNchanaa jala kumbhaasheha cha bhadrapiitham svalaNkR^itam | 2-15-4
rathashcha aastiirNaH bhaaasvataa vyaaghracharmaNaa ||

The decoration of the chariot expresses pride on a well kept and maintained vehicle befitting a prince. It is similar to the pride many people these days feel about their cars. The shiny tiger skin tells us that a tiger must have been hunted recently. In the olden days, hunting beasts of prey was considered to be a manly sport. Only the best and the most capable hunters and warriors were able to hunt these animals.

This *shloka* is given as an example of the use of chariots and to show that these beasts of prey were never kept as pets and that only their skin was used for the purposes of sitting, unlike today, when a lot of people pride themselves in keeping tigers as 'pets' and caged in zoos.

Back then, the sport of hunting these wild beasts was ideally done on horseback or on elephants. The elephant and horse were found in large numbers in Ayodhya and some references to their count are mentioned in the following chapters, especially as war animals. Can you guess the minimum number of animals mentioned in the army of Kosala Empire?

22

Chaturangi Sena

According to ancient Hindus, a robust or capable army consisted of a *chaturangi sena* or a 'four-limbed army'. The word *chatur* in Sanskrit means both clever and the number four. The word *anga* in Sanskrit means 'part or limb'. The four limbs of the *chaturangi sena* consisted of the infantry, cavalry, elephants and chariots. Both princes as well as princesses had their own armies. When Hindu princesses would marry kings or princes and move to other kingdoms, they would take their *chaturangi sena* with them or a portion of their father's *chaturangi sena*.

In the Valmiki Ramayana, Devi Sita and her sisters are given a *chaturangi sena* by their father as part of *stree dhan* or 'woman's wealth', which accompanies them to Ayodhya. For the *sena*, Valmiki specifies in Sanskrit, '*Hasti ashva ratha paadaatam*', which are the four limbs of the army. This is mentioned clearly in the *shloka* below from *sarga* 74, *Bala Kanda*, which translates to: 'King Janaka of Mithila, the one from Videha lineage, gifted elephants, horses, chariots, foot soldiers to the brides.'

अथ राजा विदेहानाम् ददौ कन्या धनम् बहु ।
गवाम् शत सहस्राणि बहूनि मिथिलेश्वरः ॥ १-७४-३
कंबलानाम् च मुख्यानाम् क्षौमान् कोटि अंबराणि च ।

हस्ति अश्व रथ पादातम् दिव्य रूपम् स्वलंकृतम् ॥ १-७४-४
ददौ कन्या शतम् तासाम् दासी दासम् अनुत्तमम् ।

hasti ashva ratha paadaatam divya ruupam
svalankR^itam || 1-74-4
dadau kanyaa shatam taasaam daasii daasam
anuttamam

From the Sanskrit word *chaturanga*, we get the word *Shatranj*, which is the Hindustani name for chess. This game was invented by a clever Brahmin to train kings, princes, generals and army chiefs in strategies of attack and defence during battle. An image of *chaturanga* or chess, the eight-squared board game invented and popularised by Hindus was shared in Part IV. This game, inspired by the real-life *chaturangi sena*, has a king and queen in the centre flanked by a minister, cavalry and an elephant on each side. Eight foot soldiers are in front of these eight warriors.

This four-limbed structure was the basic set-up of any ancient Hindu army. But the presence of limbs does not give us an idea of the number of horses or elephants actively serving in the army. In the next chapter, we will read about the divisions or large military unit formations of the army and how many animals were included in these.

23

The *akShauhiNii*

In the Valmiki Ramayana, we can learn about the number of animals in Emperor Dasharatha's army when Rishi Vishvamitra comes to take Lord Rama and his brother Lakshmana to help protect his Vedic rituals. His *dharmic* fire rituals were regularly disrupted by rakshasas or demons. But Dasharatha was not happy with the idea of sending his young sons to fight demons and offered to give Vishvamitra a full-fledged *akShauhiNii sena*.

AkShauhiNii translates to a division or a large military unit of the army. In *sarga* 20 of *Bala Kanda*, Dasharatha offers his complete military division to protect Vishvamitra's fire rituals. He also offers to personally fight with the demons along with his army instead of sending his sons.

Dasharatha's exact words are, 'Here is the full-fledged *akShauhiNii sena*, of which I am the leader and controller, and fortified by this army I will go there to encounter those demons.'

इयम् अक्षौहिणी सेना यस्य अहम् पतिः ईश्वरः |
अनया सहितो गत्वा योद्ध अहम् तैर् निशाचरैः || १-२०-३

iyam akshouhiNii sena yasya aham patiH iishwaraH |
anayaa samhito gatvaa aham taiH nishaa charaiH || 1-20-3

In the next section, we will understand how big a full fledged '*akShauhiNii*' was.

How Big Was the *akShauhiNii*?

One *pankti* or row is the first unit of the military of ancient Hindus. It consists of one chariot, one elephant, three cavalry, and five foot soldiers. As mentioned earlier, chariots, cavalry, foot soldiers and elephants form the *chaturangi sena*.

Multiples of this first unit or row becomes an *akShauhiNii sena*. One *akShauhiNii sena* consists of 21,870 chariots, 21,870 elephants, 65,610 cavalry and 109,350 foot soldiers. This four-limbed composition followed a fixed ratio of 1:1:3:5.

Multiple divisions of *akShauhiNii* were part of a king's or an emperor's army. The following calculation shows how a division of the army constituting an *akShauhiNii* is arrived at, starting from the base 'first unit or row' called *pankti* or *pattii*.

१ पत्ती (1 *pattii*) = 1 chariot + 1 elephant + 3 horses + 5 foot soldiers (base or first line)

३ पत्ती (3 *pattii*) = १ सेनामुख (1 *senamukha*)

३ सेनामुख (3 *senaamukha*) = १ गुल्म (1 *gulma*)

३ गुल्म (3 *gulma*) = १ गण (1 *gaNa*)

३ गण (3 *gaNa*) = १ वाहिनी (1 *vaahini*)

३ वाहिनी (3 *vaahinii*) = १ प्रतिमा (1 *pritamaa*)

३ प्रतिमा (3 *pritamaa*) = १ चमू (1 *chamoo*)

३ चमू (3 *chamoo*) = १ अनीकिनी (1 *aneekinii*)

१० अनीकिनी (10 *aneekinii*) = १ अक्षौहिणी (1 *akShauhiNii*)

To illustrate how an elephant would look like or participate in a *chaturangi sena*, check out the following image by an unknown artist. It depicts elephants in a battle. The painting was made between 1750 and 1770 and is from Kota, Rajasthan. It is from the Stella Kramrisch Collection at the Philadelphia Museum of Art. This image depicts two soldiers armed with spears, arrows and swords atop the elephant; the foremost soldier is the mahout who wields the elephant goad that could give a trained elephant over a hundred commands by gentle touches to different parts of the animal's body. The second soldier is the one who attacks and fights in the battle. There were 21,870 such elephants in an *akShauhiNii*.

The following image is shared to illustrate an example of cavalry. The image is a lithograph of a Maratha

warrior on a horse in India. It is from the Peter Newark
Historical Pictures collection from the Bridgeman Art
Library.

The cavalry of an akShauhiNii consisted of 65,610 such
men on horseback, with swords and weapons. Ideally,
the number of horses in an *akShauhiNii* should be much
more than 65,610 because they also pulled chariots. But
since it is not clear how many horses exactly pulled
how many chariots, we cannot accurately deduce the
exact number of horses of the Kosala army. However,
the average number of horses pulling a chariot was two
or four. Keeping this in mind, if we take a minimum

number of two horses pulling a chariot we get 43,740 (21,870 x 2). Adding this to the number of cavalry horses we get a minimum of 109,350 (43,740 + 65,610) horses in Dasharatha's *akShauhiNii*.

Therefore, we can safely say that there were a minimum of 109,350 horses and 21,870 elephants in Dasharatha's army because it is clear that he had at least one *akShauhiNii sena*. It is possible he had multiple *akShauhiNiis*, commanded by others, such as his army commanders or chiefs. Ordinarily, an emperor of his stature often kept more than one *akShauhiNii*. The Hindu *itihaasa* of Dwapara Yuga as recorded in the Mahabharata mentions that the Pandavas had an army of 7 *akShauhiNiis* and the Kauravas of 11 *akShauhiNiis*. The brutal war that occurred between the 18 *akShauhiNiis* during the battleground of Kurukshetra lasted 18 days in which most of the men of Dwapara Yuga perished.

While the minimum number of foot soldiers is mentioned in the *akShauhiNii*, the number of warriors always exceeded that count. In addition to the foot soldiers, there was at least, one warrior per horse (cavalry). This adds 65,610 to the count of 109,350 foot soldiers. In addition to cavalry and foot soldiers totalling upto 174,960, there were a minimum of two warriors atop an elephant, as depicted in the painting from Kota, which takes the minimum number of warriors to 218,700 (174,960 + 21,870 x 2).

Also, a minimum of two fighters were always on a chariot, which was led by two to four horses. This brings the count to 262,440 (218,700 + 21,870 x 2). On any chariot, one of the warriors was a charioteer controlling the horses, while the other fought. We can confirm this because the Bhagavad Gita was spoken by Lord Krishna in his role as a charioteer to Arjuna, the famous Pandava, riding the chariot in the battleground at Kurukshetra. Four horses pulled Arjuna's chariot.

But there could be more warriors on a chariot too and the number of horses could also exceed four, depending on the type of chariot. This can be inferred from the *Ayodhya Kanda* of Valmiki Ramayana, *sarga* 11, where Empress Kaikeyi speaks of saving Emperor Dasharatha's life in a dangerous battle. She speaks of it when Dasharatha has entered the *kopa bhavana* (the house of wrath) and pleads his beloved empress to reveal what is bothering her. Dasharatha is extremely distraught to see Kaikeyi lying on the floor, looking like a dead woman in torn clothes after having thrown away her chaplets and auspisious gold jewellery. The corresponding Sanskrit *shloka* with its meaning is given below.

Since it is known that Sumantra was the charioteer of Maharaja Dasharatha, from this *shloka* we can assume that there were two warriors on the chariot, namely Dasharatha and Kaikeyi, totalling the number of people on this chariot to three.

स्मर राज्ञ पुरा वृत्तं तस्मिन् दैवासुरे रणे |
तत्र चाच्यावयच्छत्रुस्तव जीवतमन्तरा || २-११-१८

तत्र चापि मया देव यत्त्वं समभिरक्षितः |
जाग्रत्या यतमानायास्ततो मे प्रादद वरौ || २-११-१९

smara rAjn purA vRRittaM tasmin daivAsure raNe |
tatra chAchyAvayachChatrustava jIvatamantarA ||

2-11-18

tatra chApi mayA deva yattvaM samabhirakShitaH |
jAgratyA yatamAnAyAstato me prAdadA varau | |

2-11-19

In the *shloka* above, Empress Kaikeyi says, 'Oh, King!
Remember what happened in the battle between
celestials and demons in the olden times. There the
enemy destroyed almost everything except your life.
Oh, King! There, I saved you. Hence, you gave boons
to myself whose vigilant efforts saved you.'

Hindu scriptures unequivocally mention that
princesses, queens, empresses and goddesses owned
armies and were fighting wars with or without their
husbands to protect their kingdoms or empires.
Valmiki Ramayana also echoes the same sentiments
and that is why Empress Kaikeyi fought alongside
her husband in brutal wars. Here, it is critical to point
out that in Hindu dharma, a man and a woman are
seen as absolute equals in stature, contrary to twisted
modern-day portrayals of women being less than
equal to men. Having said that, it was the choice of
the queen or empress to fight alongside the king or
emperor. She could also choose to not fight and look
after the kingdom or empire instead of being on the
battleground. In the Ramayana, out of the three *patta
ranis*, only Kaikeyi went to battle. Kaushalya and
Sumitra stayed back.

The equality between a man and a woman translates
to equal opportunity and right to a queen to rule the
kingdom. This thought, too, is echoed in the Valmiki
Ramayana and is expressly stated by Rishi Vashishtha in
Ayodhya Kanda, sarga 37. The *shloka* with its translation

is given below. Rishi Vashishtha speaks these lines to Empress Kaikeyi to remind her of dharma, according to which Devi Sita, the wife of Lord Rama, is not required to be banished to the forest. Instead, she has the right to rule the empire, a right that Kaikeyi's son Bharata does not have, as he is the second son of Maharaja Dasharatha.

न गन्तव्यम् वनम् देव्या सीतया शीलवर्जिते |
अनुष्ठास्यति रामस्य सीता प्रकृतमासनम् || २-३७-२३

आत्मा हि दाराः सर्वेषाम् दारसम्ग्रहवर्तिनाम् |
आत्मेयमिति रामस्य पालयिष्यति मेदिनीम् || २-३७-२४

*na gantavyam vanam devyA sItayA shIlavarjite |
anuShThAsyati rAmasya sItA prakRRitamAsanam
|| 2-37-23*

*AtmA hi dArAH sarveShAm dArasamgrahavartinAm |
Atmeyamiti rAmasya pAlayiShyati medinIm ||
2-37-24*

In the above *shlokas*, an enraged Rishi Vashishta says, 'Oh, the woman devoid of good conduct! Sita, the princess, shall not proceed to forest. She will occupy the throne which was awarded to Rama. A wife is the soul of every married man (householder). As Sita is Rama's soul, she can rule the earth.'

Rishi Vashishta speaks these lines when Lord Rama and Devi Sita have come to Emperor Dasharatha's palace to bid their final goodbyes. In the palace, Rishi Vashishtha is present along with brahmins and other important ministers, and charioteer Sumantra. He speaks these lines to dissuade Kaikeyi from further humiliating the couple and to persuade her to rethink her twin demands in order to prevent disaster from befalling the empire by making her son king and banishing Crown Prince Rama to the forest.

Men who guard or protect their wives are called householders and in the above *shloka* this phrase is denoted by the word *dArasamgrahavartinAm*. In Hindu dharma, the wife is known as the अर्धांगिनी (*ardhAMginii* or *ardhANginii*). This phrase implies that the physical body is the husband and the wife is the soul. This concept is in sync with the Samkhya philosophy of पुरुश (*purusha*) and प्रकृति (*prakRRiti*). According to this philosophy, a जीव (*jiiva*) or living being can exist only when *purusha* and *prakRRiti* combine, just like any living being can exist only when it has a soul residing in it. Death is the state when the soul leaves the body. Either one cannot exist as a *jiiva* without the other.

Therefore, this concept is translated into a marriage too, especially a lifelong monogamous marriage between a man and a woman. Prince Rama and Princess Sita had taken a lifelong vow of monogomy and so did the other three princes and princesses. This vow in Hindi is called एक पत्नि व्रत (*eka patni vrata*), which loosely translates to 'the vow of one wife' for a man and एक पति व्रत (*eka pati vrata*) or 'the vow of one husband' for a woman. Under this vow, even if a partner dies, the spouse does not take on another parter in sexual or marital capacity.

Therefore, in the above *shloka*, Rishi Vashishtha is referring to this philosophy when he says that Princess Sita has the right to rule the earth. This negates the right of Prince Bharata to the throne of Kosala, as he is the younger brother of Lord Rama. Princess Sita, the wife of the crown prince, cannot be banished to the forest either because the immoral punishment meted to Lord Rama does not apply to her. Instead, she should rule the empire in his absence.

Rishi Vashishtha also mentions that Crown Princess Sita will rule the earth since the descendents of the Ikshwaku clan are its legitimate rulers. Ikshwaku is the son of Manu, the progenitor of mankind, and, therefore, Crown Princess Sita becomes the rightful heir to the throne of the earth, that is, Kosala Empire in the absence of her husband Crown Prince Rama, the scion of Iskhwaku.

The above example of the wife being the soul of husband and, therefore, possessing the right to run a household, a kingdom or an empire usually applies to the first wife of the husband, in case he has more than one wife. It is she who is the धर्म पत्नि (*dharma patni*) or the lawfully-wedded wife without whose presence a man cannot partake in vedic rituals to uphold the path of dharma. In special cases, like that of emperors who had numerous wives, the concept of *patta ranis* or empresses existed to outline which of the chosen wives would become empresses. This concept has been explained in Part IV with examples of Maharaja Dasharatha's *patta ranis*. Since Empress Kausalya was the *dharma patni* and the senior most *patta rani*, Lord Rama was first in line to the throne of the Kosala Empire.

Through the stories of battles and boons of the Valmiki Ramayana, we have deduced not only the rights of women to the throne but also the structure and composition of an *akShauhiNii*. We have also determined the minimum number of horses and elephants in the army of Kosala Empire. In the next chapter, we will read about the other animals that abound in Ayodhya.

24

Useful Animals Abounding Ayodhya

In the 5th *sarga* of *Bala Kanda*, Valmiki mentions all the animals he considers useful when describing the city of Ayodhya. He says that these useful animals are abundant in the city. The following *shloka* translates to, 'That Ayodhya is an impassable one for trespassers, or for others invaders, owing to her impassable and profound moats, and she is abounding with horses, camels, likewise with cows and donkeys.'

दुर्ग गंभीर परिखाम् दुर्गाम् अन्यैः दुरासदम् |
वाजीवारण संपूर्णम् गोभिः उष्ट्रैः खरैः तथा || १-५-१३

*durga gambhiira parikhaam durgaam anyaiH
duraasadam |
vaajii vaarana sampuurNam gobhiH uSTraiH
kharaiH tatha || 1-5-13*

The first part of the *shloka* has been described in much detail in Part III of the book and in the second part, Valmiki gives us the list of useful animals: cows and bulls, horses, elephants, donkeys and camels. They are useful not only for farming but also used for pulling carts and chariots. The cow, considered sacred in Hindu culture, is an animal that gives us milk, dairy products like ghee, paneer (cheese), curd and various other delectable foods (prepared using milk products).

After this cursory mention in *sarga* 5, Valmiki describes these animals, their importance and their breeding in *sarga* 6. The description of imported horses and breeding of elephants is given in great detail in the Valmiki Ramayana.

Sage Valmiki says that there is no home that is devoid of cows or horses in Ayodhya. He mentions that in *shloka* 7 of *sarga* 6, which translates into English as follows: 'None with meagre accumulations is there in that great city and no householder is there without unearned means, and without cows, horses, monies or cereals and who could not sustain his family.'

न अल्प संनिचयः कश्चिद् आसीत् तस्मिन् पुरोत्तमे |
कुटुंबी यो हि असिद्धर्थः अगवा अश्व धन धान्यवान् || १-६-७

na alpa sannichaya kaschit aasiit tasmin pura uttame I
kuTumbii yaH hi a siddha artha a gaava ashva dhana
dhanyavaan || 1-6-7

This *shloka* suggests that there were no poor in Ayodhya, and even the least affluent people owned cows and horses. Also, a cow is sacred for all Hindus and is treated as a family member. Since cows provide various edible products and horses are mostly used for transport, this signifies that no one in Ayodhya was without basic nutrition or transportation.

Another interesting point to note here is that access to good nutrition, specifically dairy products, is a contributor to height in humans as mentioned by the WHO (refer to Part III). Here, Valmiki clearly states that the poorest of the poor in Ayodhya had a cow at home. Therefore, one can assume that the residents of the district must have been taller than the average Indian of today.

Because of the reverence given to the cow and the presence of many varieties of native Indian cows, Hindus in the past did not import cows to Ayodhya. However, other animals were imported. Can you guess the animals that were imported?

25

Importing Horses and Hippopotamuses

One of the best and fastest means of transport in olden times were horses. Before the invention of the combustion-engine car, people all over the globe would either travel on horseback, horse-led carriages or chariots. In Ayodhya, everything man-made is readily available in the district itself. Sage Valmiki clearly mentions that all possible machines were invented and constructed in Ayodhya. Many inventors, mechanics and sculptors were citizens of Kosala and resided in Ayodhya. The word for machines in Sanskrit is *yantra*. There were many markets in Ayodhya that sold indigenously manufactured *yantras*. This is explicitly mentioned in the following *shloka* from the *Bala Kanda, sarga* 5.

कपाट तोरणवर्ती सु विभक्त अन्तरापणाम् |
सर्व यंत्र अयुधवतीम् उषिताम् सर्व शिल्पिभिः || १-५-१०

kapATa toraNavartI su vibhakta antarApaNAm |
sarva yaMtra ayudhavatIm uShitAm sarva shilpibhiH ||

1-5-10

Sage Valmiki in the *shloka* says: 'That city is surrounded with gateways and archways; the front yards of buildings are well laid; it lodges all kinds of machinery, weaponry and craftsmen, and Maharaja Dasharatha dwells in such a city.'

But horses do not seem to be Ayodhya's forte and excellent horses were imported from other kingdoms. They were such fantastic imports that Valmiki does not shy away from calling them *hari haya uttamaiH*. The Sanskrit word '*haya*' means horse. *Hari-haya* is the name of Indra's horse and the Sun God's horses are also called *hari-haya*. *Hari-haya* also means golden-coloured (hay-coloured) horse. The Sanskrit word *uttamaiH* means exemplary or excellent.

Surprisingly, apart from horses, Ayodhya also imported river horses, commonly known as hippopotamuses. Details about the horses imported into Ayodhya are given in *shloka* 22 of *sarga* 6, *Bala Kanda*. This *shloka* would translate to, 'From Kaambhoja and Baahlika kingdoms, the best horses are imported. From the kingdom of Vanaayu horses, and from near the rivers of Sindhu, hippopotamuses are imported into Ayodhya. These excellent imported horses and hippopotamuses are like the *ucChiashravas*, the horse of Indra. These horses and hippopotamuses are found in plenty in the district.' This description is given by the Gita Press version of the Valmiki Ramayana.

कांभोज विषये जातैः बाह्लिकैः च हय उत्तमैः |
वनायुजैः नदीजैः च पूर्णा हरिहय उत्तमैः || १-६-२२

kaambhoja viSaye jaataiH baahlikaiH cha haya uttamaiH |
vanaayu jaiH nadii jaH cha puurNaa hari haya uttamaiH | | 1-6-22

Indra's horse *ucChiashravas* was born during *samudra manthana* (the churning of the ocean) in Hindu Cosmology. He is considered the king of horses. It is possible that Valmiki meant both that the golden-coloured horses as well as other excellent horses were imported in Ayodhya.

The word *ucChiashravas* in Sanskrit is a conjunction of two words that could have a few meanings. *UcCai* means 'high/tall' in Sanskrit. The word *shravas* translates to 'ears, sound, or swift course, rapid motion and gushing forward'. Therefore, the name could denote possible meanings like: tall-eared horse, a horse that neighs loudly or a swift horse, (almost) flying horse. These adjectives could also apply to a hippopotamus, which not only has a very loud voice but also swims rapidly in water.

Possible reasons for calling *ucChiashravas* a flying horse could be because the Hindu *Yoga Shastras* mention that the medium for sound to travel is *akaash* (space). Since sound travels fast, the word *shravas* has multiple meanings attached to it, including that of flying (movement in space). The basic meaning of *shravas*, however, remains 'hearing/listening'.

According to Hindus, creation is made up of five elements: Earth or *Prithvi*, Water or *Jal*, Fire or *Agni*, Air or *Vayu*, Space or *Akaash*. These elements contain five different characteristics and each accounts for a different faculty, just like sound is accorded to *Akaash*. For yogis (followers of *Yoga Shastras*), the knowledge of the five elements allows them to understand the laws of nature. While translating or interpreting Sanskrit words from Hindu Cosmology, it is important to keep these factors in mind, as they are helpful in determining the relationship between outwardly distinct and multiple meanings of the same word.

According to Hindu Cosmology, *ucChiashravas,* the flying horse, is white in colour. On the other hand, the horses of the Sun God are golden. With these descriptions, we can assume that with the word *hari-haya,* Valmiki implies both golden and/or the best of horses like those of the Sun God and Indra.

While one can understand the importing of horses, what could be the possible reason for importing the hippopotamus?

The Possible Use of Hippopotamus

While the English commentators and translators fail to mention hippopotamuses being imported, it is clearly mentioned in the Gita Press Valmiki Ramayana that hippopotamuses were indeed imported into Ayodhya. The word used by Valmiki for the hippopotamus is *nadiijaH,* which, in Sanskrit, means river-borne. This word is attributed to the lotus, the hippopotamus and the plants and reeds found in river waters. For this reason, the hippopotamus is commonly called a river horse or a *dariyai ghoda* in Hindi.

Similar to the word *nadiijaH* meaning hippopotamus, Sanskrit is full of words that include the suffix *ja,* which means 'born of'; in fact, even Devi Sita is called *Kshitija,* which means earth-born or found in earth. According to certain stories of Hindu *itihaasa,* Devi Sita was found by her father Maharaja Janak while ploughing a field.

It is pertinent to mention that the hippopotamus or the river horse does not inhabit any water body except slow-moving rivers and lakes. While horses move fast on land, these lumbering giants are speedy swimmers in lakes and slow-moving rivers. Today, India does not have any hippopotamuses outside of confined and protected areas, though intriguingly enough, hippopotamus fossils have been found around river basins in India.

According to an article in *The Hindu* newspaper written by Awasti Pacha in January 2019, a hippopotamus fossil in India was excavated in 2003 by Rajeev Patnaik of Punjab University and Parth R. Chauhan of the Indian Institute of Science Education and Research, Mohali. They had spent days studying the fossiliferous silt near the Narmada River and Chauhan stated, 'We believed that the species was older than 50,000 years and did not study it fully. Recently, I analysed the date using accelerator mass spectroscopy in Taiwan. It revealed that the specimen was quite young and could possibly be among the last ones that lived in India.'

At this point, it is fascinating to note that the hippopotamus fossil was found near the Narmada River, the lifeline river of Madhya Pradesh and Gujarat.

The article further quotes a paper published in *Quaternary International*, mentioning that the dating studies showed that this hippopotamus lived during a 'particularly dry period in the late quaternary' period (15,000–16,000 years ago). Severe drought in South Asia and weak Indian monsoons might have led to its extinction.

According to Hindu *itihaasa*, there was a state called Maha Kausala or Maha Kosala, which was located in modern-day Madhya Pradesh. Today, this is the area around the upper or eastern reaches of the Narmada river valley with the Vindhya Ranges as the northern boundary of the region. Maha Kausala or Greater Kausala was a state as old as the Kosala Empire of Maharaja Dasharatha and these two states most likely shared a border. Maharaja Dasharatha's first wife, Kausalya, comes from the state of Maha Kaushala. The name *Kausalya* in Sanskrit literally translates to 'belonging to the people of the Kosala' or 'daughter of the prince/king of Kosala'. She is the mother of Lord Rama. This is the typical manner in which the queens or empresses were addressed in the past. Likewise, the name *Kaikeyi* means the daughter of the prince/king of the Kekaya.

Coming back to the possible reasons for importing hippopotamuses, unlike the citizens of present-era India, those in ancient Bharat perhaps knew the benefits of hippopotamuses. This is why Valmiki mentions it in the Ramayana. The hippopotamus's dung is incredibly useful for the ecosystem of rivers and lakes because they feed on land and defecate in water, depositing vast amounts of nutrients in the water. The dung also feeds certain river fish.

Following is an image of a hippopotamus in water from San Diego Zoo captured by user cloudzilla on Wikipedia.

In Part III of this book, we have already covered how the Sarayu River provided water for the citizens of Ayodhya and also fed its moats. Valmiki Ramayana states that Sarayu's sweet water tasted like sugarcane juice. Valmiki also states that the water was used to produce paddy in the district. The sweetness could be owed to the fact that the river's source is Nanda Kot of the Himalayan mountain ranges and many rivers merge into Sarayu before it hits the plains. Undoubtedly, Sarayu would be carrying large amounts of silt with it too.

But once the river water reaches the plains, dams, canals or moats are constructed and the nutrient quotient of the water depletes inevitably. Farming requires water that not only carries adequate silt but that it is also constantly kept nutrient-rich. This is perhaps where the hippopotamuses came into play and kept the waters of Ayodhya rich in nutrients.

Apart from paddy, there are also numerous mango groves and gardens in Ayodhya. The presence of both shows that the waters of the Sarayu were cleverly inducted in Ayodhya. Also, the waters of Sarayu fed the moat of Ayodhya, which is full of lotus and crocodiles (if we go by Kautilya's instructions).

Combining the above-mentioned facts and keeping in mind a wholesome picture of Ayodhya, it becomes evident that the hippopotamus was a likely source of nourishment to the waters used in paddy fields, moats, mango groves and the gardens of Ayodhya. Since its fossil has been found in the Maha Kosala area as well, it can be supposed that either Maha Kosala imported them too or they naturally spread from the adjoining Empire of Kosala. We can consider this, as there is no written record of such imports to Maha Kosala, but these records exist in the Ramayana for Kosala Empire.

The information about plenty of water available in Ayodhya to grow water-intensive paddy, feed the gardens and provide for mangoes is given in *shlokas* mentioned below. Details about paddy grown in Ayodhya are given in *sarga* 5 of *Bala Kanda*. The *shloka* translates to: 'The housing is very dense and there is no place or ground unutilised, and all are constructed on well-levelled lands, and *shaali* rice-grain is plentiful while the drinking water tastes like sugarcane juice.'

गृह गाढाम् अविच्छिद्राम् सम भूमौ निवेशिताम् ।
शालि तण्डुल संपूर्णाम् इक्षु काण्ड रसः उदकाम् ॥१-५-१७

gR^iha gaaDhaam a vi cChidraam sama bhuumau
niveshitaam |
shaali taNDula sampuurNaam ikshu kaNDa rasa
udakaam || 1-5-17

According to this *shloka*, a unique kind of paddy named *shaali taNDula* is grown. The word *taNDula* in Sanskrit means 'uncooked rice grain'. The English translations have just mentioned this as fine-grained rice. Some translations have ignored the word *shaali* and instead mentioned it as 'lots of rice'. Some have translated both *shaali* and taNDula to rice. But there is a big difference in Sanskrit between the two words. While composing advanced poetry, it would have been rather careless of a learned poet like Valmiki to write: 'rice rice full, sweet waters like sugarcane.'

Therefore, it is obvious that *shaali* was a type of rice he refers to. In a commentary included in the Gita Press, this has been clearly translated as a type of rice called *jaDhana*, which is a distinct variety of paddy whose saplings are uprooted from one area and planted in another. This paddy is densely sown in the month of *Ashadh*, one of the starting months of monsoon, according to the Hindu calendar. When the plants are one or two feet tall, the farmers uproot them and replant them in the middle fields along the banks of the river or in farms that have knee-high water. References to *shaali* rice are also found in Ayurvedic texts like *Charak Samhita*, where it is considered the highest quality of rice.

After the mention of the special *shaali* rice grown in Ayodhya, the presence of mango groves and gardens is mentioned in the same *sarga*. The following *shloka* conveys, 'The city of Ayodhya accommodates groups of danseuses and theatrical personnel, and she is surrounded everywhere with the gardens and mango groves.'

वधू नाटक सन्घैः च संयुक्ताम् सर्वतः पुरीम् |
उद्यान आम्र वणोपेताम् महतीम् साल मेखलाम् || १-५-१२

vadhuu naaTaka sanghaiH cha samyuktaam sarvataH puriim |
udyaana aamra vana upetaam mahatiim saala mekhalaam ||1-5-12

Now that we have read about hippopotamuses, their possible uses and also about the crops grown in Ayodhya, let us move on to another important animal, the elephant. Can you guess where the elephants were imported from in Ayodhya?

26

Importing and Breeding of Elephants

A long with horses and hippopotamuses, elephants were also brought to Ayodhya from different parts of Bharat, such as the Vindhya, Himalayan and Sahya Ranges, in the Ramayanic Era. They were then interbred in the district of Ayodhya.

For the elephants, in the following *shloka* from *sarga 6* of *Bala Kanda*, Sage Valmiki says: 'Born in Vindhya Mountains, and also from Himalayan regions, mighty are the elephants fully *musth* and fattened ones, and most powerful in their strength and each in similitude is a huge mountain.'

विंध्य पर्वतजैः मत्तैः पूर्णा हैमवतैः अपि |
मदान्वितैः अतिबलैः मातङ्गैः पर्वतौपमैः || १-६-२३

vindhya parvata jaiH mattaiH puurNa haimavataiH api |
mada anvitaiH ati balaiH maatangaiH parvata
upamaiH ||1-6-23

Sage Valmiki uses the term *mada anvitaiH* as a feature of these mountain-like elephants. This term is associated with *musth* or *mada* flowing from their temples. *Musth* is the period of the year during which elephants are sexually active. This is similar to the 'rut' of animals like deer and sheep. In the case of elephants, Valmiki is hinting that these elephants are in their sexual prime when imported. Another reason to mention this is to emphasise that an elephant would be imported in its sexual prime for the purposes of breeding. It is also to be noted that these *mada anvitaiH* or passionately intoxicated or excited (with sexual desire) elephants are extremely tricky to manage and train.

Continuing to discuss the importing and breeding of elephants, Valmiki adds in the next *shloka*, 'High bred from the classes of Airavata, the Elephant of Lord Indra, from classes of Mahapadma, Anjana and Vamana, too... are the elephants (of Ayodhya).'

इरावत कुलीनैः च महापद्म कुलैः तथा |
अंजनादपि निष्क्रान्तैः वामनादपि च द्विपैः || १-६-२४

iraavata kuliinaiH cha mahaapadma kulaiH tatha |
anjanaat api niSkraantaiH vaamanaat api cha
dvipaiH || 1-6-24

The names that Valmiki mentions are elephants mentioned in Hindu Cosmology. He says that the elephants imported are from the breed or clan of *airavat* or *iraavata*, the best amongst elephants, who is the vehicle of choice for the king of Gods, Indra. Vamana and Anjana are two grand elephants who support the earth according to Hindu Cosmology. Their descendents are imported and bred in Ayodhya.

According to Hindu Cosmology, there are four grand elephants supporting the four corners of the earth whose names are given in the Valmiki Ramayana in *sarga* 40 of *Bala Kanda*. They are: Virupaksha (east), Mahaapadma (south), Saumanasa (west) and Bhadra (north). Bhadra is mentioned as being as white as snow.

Further to *shloka* 24 mentioned above, in *shloka* 25 Sage Valmiki states, 'The capital city (of Ayodhya) was always full of intoxicated elephants and mountain-like elephants bred mainly from three classes, namely Bhadra from Himalayan regions, Mandra from Vindhya mountain ranges and Mriga from Sahya Mountain ranges. And inter-bred among these three main classes are Bhadra-Mandra, Mandra-Mriga, Bhadra-Mriga and the like.'

भद्रैः मन्द्रैः मृगैः च एव भद्र मन्द्र मृगैः थथा |
भद्र मन्द्रैः भद्र मृगैः मृग मन्द्रैः च सा पुरी || १-६-२५
नित्य मत्तैः सदा पूर्णा नागैः अचल सन्निभैः |

*bhadraiH mandraiH mR^igaiH cha eva bhadra
mandra mR^igaiH tathaa |
bhadra mandraiH bhadra mR^ igaiH mR^iga
mandraiH cha saa purii || 1-6-24
nitya mattaiH sadaa puurNaa naagaiH achala
sannibhaiH |*

Elephants were used for lifting and doing heavy work, including building homes and palaces, apart from taking part in royal processions and wars. According to Hindus, the different classes of elephants were useful for various purposes. The Bhadra variety were used for the king's ride, and called *Bhadra Gaja*. It was a state elephant and given high honours. The Mandra and

Mriga breeds were tamed, so they could be used in wars or as rides of nobility other than the king. They were also used for lifting and carrying jobs.

Towards the end of the Ramayana, Valmiki mentions that during the coronation of Lord Rama, 9,000 elephants followed him to the ceremony. In a *shloka* from *sarga* 128 of *Ayodhya Kanda,* he says, 'Assuming human forms and adorned with all types of ornaments, monkeys sallied forth, mounting on 9,000 elephants.'

From this, one could (perhaps) deduce that the minimum number of Mandra and Mriga classes of elephants were 9,000 in number in Ayodhya. Previously, in the chapter discussing the *akshouhiNii,* we had established that there were 21,870 elephants in the army.

नवनागसहस्राणि ययुरास्थाय वानराः |
मानुषन् विग्रहन् कृत्वा सर्वाभरणभूषिताः || ६-१२८-३२

navanaagasahasraani yayuH aasthaaya vaanaraaH |
maanuShaM vigraham kR^itvaa
sarvaabharaNabhuuShitaaH || 6-128-32

In *Ayodhya Kanda,* when Lord Rama almost became the king, there is a beautiful *shloka* that talks about the animals waiting for him. Sage Valmiki says, 'A white bull, a white horse, and a mighty and beautiful elephant which was fit to be mounted by kings were readily waiting.' This must be the Bhadra breed, as it is the ride of the royals. These animals were waiting for Prince Rama because he was going to be crowned king and

then be of service to him. The *shloka* from *sarga* 15 is
shown below.

पाण्डुरश्च वृषः सज्जः पाण्डुरोऽस्वश्च सुस्थितः || २-१५-११
प्रसृतश्च गजः श्रीमानौपवाह्यः प्रतीक्षते |

*paaN^DuraH cha vR^ishhaH sajjaH paaN^DuraH
ashvaH cha susthitaH || 2-15-11
prasR^itaH cha gajaH shriimaan oupaaahyaH
pratiikshhate |*

Valmiki, in a later *shloka,* also narrates about Rama's
personal elephant. The following *shloka* is from
sarga 15, *Ayodhya Kanda.* Valmiki states, at the entrance
of the personal royal palace of Prince Rama, 'Here
(Dasharatha's charioteer) Sumantra saw a beautiful
elephant called Shatrunjaya with a highly elevated
body—Rama's royal conveyance. It was like a great
cloud and a mountain. It was intoxicated, uncontrollable
and intolerable.'

ततो महामेघमहीधराभं |
प्रभिन्नमत्यङ्शमत्यसह्याम् |
रामोपवाह्याम् रुचिरम् ददर्श |
शत्रुम्जयं नागमुदग्रकायम् || २-१५-४७

*tataH mahaamegha mahiidharaabham |
prabhinnam atyaN^kusham asahyam |
raamopavaahyam ruchiram dadarsha |
shatrunjayam naagamudagrakaayam || 2-15-47*

This *shloka* does not make clear whether Shatrunjaya is white, but this is the same elephant given to Sugreeva to ride to Lord Rama's coronation ceremony. Sugreeva was made the king of Kishkindha by Lord Rama and his subjects were *vanaras*. Lord Rama in *Kishkindha Kanda* also refers to Sugreeva as *sakha*. *Sakha* in Sanskrit means a very close or a dear friend who knows the matters of the heart. Therefore, to honour Sugreeva, this elephant was given to him for his ride to the ceremony.

Now that we have discussed elephants, horses and hippopotamuses of Ayodhya in detail, let's find out about the birds in Ayodhya.

27

The Birds of Ayodhya

Royals of ancient Ayodhya used to keep beautiful large and small birds as pets. One can assume birds like the pigeons, crows, bulbuls, mynahs and sparrows were in abundance in the Ramayanic Era, considering they are in plenty even today. While these birds are not explicitly mentioned, various other birds are mentioned as being reared in palaces of Ayodhya.

One could hear the sound of birds like the *kraunch*, *saras* and *hans* coming from the palaces. *Hans* or *hamsa* in Sanskrit is the swan. *Kraunch* is the common crane (Grus grus), while s*aras* is a non-migratory crane called the Indian crane (Grus antigone). Some commentators have translated the *kraunch* as a curlew too. The *kraunch* is specifically mentioned as the common crane in the book *Birds in Sanskrit Literature* written by K.N. Dave, published by Motilal Banarasidass. But, according to my research, the curlew might be the bird called *kraunch*.

According to Hindu scriptures, the seven islands on Earth are जम्बूद्वीप (*JambUdvIpa)* or the island of Jambuu, प्लक्षद्वीप (*PlakShadvIpa)* or the island of Plaksh, शाल्मलद्वीप (*ShAlmaladvIpa)* or the island of Shaalmal, कुशद्वीप (*KushadvIpa)* or the island of Kusha, क्रौंचद्वीप (*KrauMchadvIpa)* or the island of Kraunch, शाकद्वीप (*ShAkadvIpa)* or the island of Shaak and पुष्करद्वीप (*PuShkaradvIpa)* or the island of Pushkar.

Here, the fifth island is called Kraunch. It is said that this island is surrounded by an ocean of buttermilk. Here, the word 'island' signifies continent. This is mentioned in the *Vishnu Purana, Dvitiya Ansha, Chaturtha Adhyaya, shloka* 57.

क्रौञ्चद्वीपः समुद्रेण दधिमण्डोदकेन च ।
आवृतः सर्वतः क्रौञ्चद्वीपतुल्येन मानतः ॥

krau~nchadvIpaH samudreNa dadhimaNDodakena cha |
AvRRitaH sarvataH krau~nchadvIpatulyena
mAnataH ||

The above *shloka* implies that the island of Kraunch is in the ocean like it has been churned, just as curd is churned to create buttermilk.

On visually observing and studying the seven continents of Earth, only Antartica seems to be shaped like a curlew. This is evident in the various aerial images of the continent. The shape changes a bit owning to the melting ice, but the curlew is seen prominently eitherways. Antartica owes its bird shape to the strategically placed Transantartic Mountain ranges and the Antartic Peninsula. In the following images, one can observe the shape of a sitting curlew and this shape does not resemble the common crane.

The first image of Antartica is rotated towards the right, so that the image of a sitting curlew can be seen clearly. The second image of Antartica outlines the mountains because of which Antartica takes it shape. The first image is from pikrepo and the second image is by krill oil, both sourced from Wikipedia. The third image is of an actual curlew. This image is by Eugene Cheah, Wikipedia, and features the Eurasian Curlew or the Common Curlew (*Numenius Arquata Orientalis*).

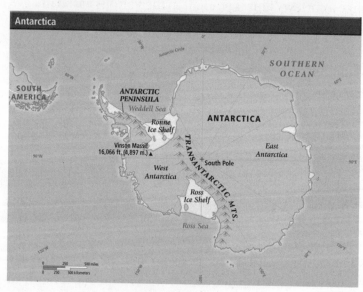

Another interesting fact mentioned in the *Vishnu Purana* about Kraunch Island is that it is surrounded by an ocean of buttermilk. This may sound strange and absurd because one assumes these definitions to be limited to the taste or texure of the ocean. But this is not the case and this definition describes the view of the ocean and continent of Antartica from a considerable height.

On careful observation of aerial images of Antartica and its ocean, the broken, floating and melting ice in the ocean definitely resembles curd or buttermilk. In the absence of aerial photography, the fact that Antartica is shaped like a Common Curlew and its ocean looks like buttermilk could never be substantiated. What is intriguing to note is that these facts could only be observed from space or from a considerable height. Without an aircraft, this description of Antartica was impossible thousands of years ago when the *Vishnu Purana* was written. We have to also remember that the Western world 'discovered' Antartica only in 1820 in an expedition led by the Russians. Therefore, there were no maps or images circulated in India prior to this.

When we add up these small facts about the numbers, shapes and sizes of continents and the construction of homes resembling the shapes of *vimaanas*, it becomes quite clear that people in the ancient past indeed flew around earth and even traversed space (also called darkness in Hindu scriptures). It is only the arrogance and ignorance of humans of today that make them believe that they are the only intelligent species in the universe. This is similar to the arrogance displayed in the past when Galelio Galilei tried to tell the West that the Earth revolved around the sun and not the other way around. For speaking such truths, he was to be executed by the church. Sadly, even with the presence of numerous facts, many similar fallacies still grip the human mind today, wherein, some people believe that the Earth is flat and at the centre of the universe and that aliens are unintelligent creatures who want to destroy human civilisation, the latter specifically perpetuated by Western movies.

Now that it is clear that the *Vishnu Purana* was written in a time when there were means to observe Earth from above via some kind of space or air travel because of which the ancient Hindus named Antartica as the Curlew Continent or *KrauMchadvIpa*. This implies that at the palaces too, it was the curlew and not the common crane when Valmiki mentions that *kraunch* can be seen.

Sage Valmiki also states that the beautiful palace of Empress Kaikeyi used to rear birds like peacock and parrot. According to the *shlokas* mentioned below, the voices of the *kraunch* and the swans were heard in the palace. It is most likely that these birds were reared in the palace gardens.

The *shlokas* describing the birds of Kaikeyi's palace are grouped together with the description of her palace in the Valmiki Ramayana. These *shlokas* describe the palace in great detail. A complete description of the palace is given in Part IV of this book.

According to these *shlokas*, when Emperor Dasharatha enters the inner apartments of Kaikeyi's prosperous abode, it is filled with parrots and peacocks, reverberating with the cries of *kraunchas* and swans, and sounds of musical instruments. The *shloka* describing the birds in Sanskrit says, *shukabarahiNa samyuktam krauncha hamsa rutaayutam*. The Sanskrit *shlokas* are mentioned below.

शुकबर्हिणसंयुक्तं क्रौञ्चहंसरुतायुतम् ॥ २-१०-१२
वादित्ररवसंघुष्टं कुब्जावामनिकायुतम् ।
लतागृहैश्चित्रगृहैश्चम्पकाशोकशोभितैः ॥ २-१०-१३
दान्तराजत सौवर्णवेदिकाभिस्समायुतम् ।
नित्यपुष्पफलैर्वृक्षैर्वापीभिश्रोपशोभितम् ॥ २-१०-१४
दान्तराजतसौवर्णैः संवृतं परमासनैः ।
विविधैयैर्रत्नपानैश्च भक्ष्यैश्चवि विधैरपि ॥ २-१०-१५
उपपन्नं महार्हैश्च भूषितैस्त्रिदिवोपमम् ।
तत्प्रविश्य महाराजः स्वमन्तःपुरमृद्धिमत् ॥ २-१०-१६
न ददर्श प्रियां राजा कैकेयीं शयनोत्तमे ।

shukabarahiNa samyuktam krauncha hamsa
rutaayutam || 2-10-12
vaaditrarava sanghushhtam kubjaa vaamanikaayutam |
lataagR^ihaiH cha chitragR^ihaiH cha champaka
ashoka shobhitaiH || 2-10-13
daantaraajata souvarNa vedikaabhiH samaayutam |
nitya pushhpa phalaiH vR^ikshhaiH vaapiibhiH cha
upashobhitam || 2-10-14
daantaraajata sauvarNaiH samvR^itam
paramaasanaiH |
vividhaiH aunapaanaiH cha bhakshhaiH cha
vividhaiH api || 2-10-15
upapannam mahaarhaiH cha bhuushhitaiH
stridivopamam |
tat pravishya mahaaraajaH svam antaH puram
Riddhimat || 2-10-16
nadadarsha priyam raajaa kaikeyiim shayauottame |

The Sanskrit word *shuka* means parrot and *barahiNa*
means a peacock. In order to illustrate the birds at the
palace of Empress Kaikeyi, the following images have
been shared.

शुकबर्हिणसंयुक्तं क्रौञ्चहंसरुतायुतम्

Below is an image of *hansaaH* or swans in water by Trudie Roden, found on Pexels.

The following is the image of a pair of *kraunchas* wading in shallow waters. This image was captured by Burkhard Leuling, and uploaded on Pixabay. Like the *sarus* cranes, the *krauncha* also displays an indefinite monogamous pair bonding. The *krauncha* or curlew has a distinct call, which can be heard at night or at dusk, as it is a nocturnal bird that nests on the ground. They have a rather interesting courtship behaviour where the male stamps its feet with its wings outstretched, its tail upright and its neck stretched forward while calling out loudly. These calls last for an hour and then repeated till the male is noticed by a female curlew who shows interest in him. This courtship might be a rare sight since these birds mate for life and they can live upto 30 years.

Similarly, a detailed description of Lord Rama's palace in Ayodhya is given below. It was also covered in Part IV. These *shlokas* describe the presence of birds by saying that Lord Rama's palace was crowded with various kinds of birds. This signifies that he had various birds as pets whom he reared at his personal quarters though these *shlokas* only mention two types of birds singing. Here Sage Valmiki says, '*saarasaiH mayuuraishcha vinadadbhiH*', which translates to '*saruses* and peacocks were singing sweetly'.

महाकवाटपिहितं वितर्दिशतशोभितम् || २-१५-३२
काञ्चनप्रतिमैकाग्रं मणिविद्रुमतोरणम् |
शारदाभ्रघनप्रख्यं दीप्तं मेरुगुहोपमम् || २-१५-३३
मणिभिर्वरमाल्यानां सुमहद्भिरलंकृतम् |
मुक्तामणिभिराकीर्ण चन्धनागुरुभूषितम् || २-१५-३४
गन्धान्मनोज्ञान् विसृजद्भद्रार्दुरं शिखरं यथा |
सारसैश्च मयूरैश्च विनदद्भिर्विराजितम् || २-१५-३५
सुकृतेहामृगाकीर्ण सुकीर्ण भक्तिभिस्तथा |
मन्श्रक्षुश्च भूतानामाददत्तिग्मतेजसा || २-१५-३६

चन्द्रभास्करसंकाशम् कुबेरभवनोपमम् ।
महेन्द्रधामप्रतिमं नानापक्षिसमाकुलम् ॥ २-१५-३७
मेरुशृङ्गसमम् सूतो रामवेश्म ददर्श ह ।
उपस्थितैः समाकीर्णम् जनैरञ्जलिकारिभिः ॥ २-१५-३८
उपादाय समाक्रान्तैस्तथा जानपदैर्जनैः ।
रामाभिषेकसुमुखैरुन्मुखैः समलम्कृतम् ॥ २-१५-३९
महामेघसमप्रख्यमुदग्रं सुविभूषितम् ।
नानारत्नसमाकीर्णं कुब्जकैरातकावृतम् ॥ २-१५-४०

mahaakavaata pihitam vitardhishata shobhitam ||
2-15-32
kaaN^chana pratimaikaagram maNividruma toranam |
sharadaabhraghanaprakhyam diiptam
meruguhopamam || 2-15-33
maNibhiH varamaalyaanaam sumadbhiH
alankR^itam |
muktaamaNibhiH aakiirNam
chandanaagurubhuushhitam || 2-15-34
gandhaan manojJNaan visR^ijat daduram shikharam
yathaa |
saarasaiH mayuuraishcha vinadadbhiH viraajitam ||
2-15-35
sukR^itehaa mR^igaakiirNam sukiirNam bhaktibhiH
tatha |
manaH chakshhushcha bhuutaanaam aadadat
tigmatejasaa || 2-15-36
chandrabhaaskaraa sankaasham kubera
bhavanopamana |
mahendra chaama pratimam
nanaapakshhisamaakulam || 2-15-37
merushR^ingasamam suutaH raamaveshma
dadarshaH |

upasthitaiH samaakiirNam janaiH aN^jalikaaribhiH
|| 2-15-38
upadaaya samaakrantaiH tathaa jaanapadaiH janiH I
raamaabhishheka sumukhaiH unmkhaiH
samalankR^itam || 2-15-39
mahaameghasamaprakhyam udagram
suvibhuushhitam |
naanaaratnasamaakiirNam kubja
kairaatakaavR^itam || 2-15-40

Below is a beautiful image of a dancing Indian peacock captured by Kalyan Varma on kalyanvarma.net. These peacocks and peahens were in plenty at the palace of Lord Rama and Devi Sita.

Given below is an image titled 'Dancing *sarus* cranes of India' by user Asheesh Mamgain on Wikipedia. These birds can be easily distinguished from other cranes because of their grey colour and the contrasting red head and upper neck.

The *sarus* in India has been favoured as a pet, along with the *kraunch*. The *sarus* is the tallest flying bird in the world. It prefers to nest on ground or in shallow waters. There were numerous water pools in Kaikeyi's palace. We can assume the same for Prince Rama's palace, though the presence of water pools is not explicitly mentioned. These birds most likely nested and waded in and around those pools.

The *sarus* cranes are considered symbols of marital fidelity, as they are believed to mate for life and mourn the loss of their mates even to the point of starving to death. Is it, therefore, on purpose that Valmiki specifically mentions these birds singing in the palace of Lord Rama and Devi Sita, as both of them had vowed to commit to each other for their entire lives?

The *kraunch* is also known to mate for life following an elaborate courtship. It is also interesting to note that the clever Valmiki chooses to name this bird specifically at Dasharatha and Kaikeyi's palace. Is its unique courtship the reason why the *krauncha* is mentioned with regards to their palace, since Emperor Dasharatha was forever besotted by Empress Kaikeyi?

One can only speculate about the truth and the implied reason behind mentioning certain birds because only Valmiki knows the truth and the reason. As inheritors of this beautiful and layered poem, we can only assume.

To sum up this chapter, a list of the birds found in Ayodhya's palaces is as follows:

Parrots

Peacocks

Curlews

Swans

Saruses or Indian Cranes

In the next chapter, we will discover what other pets were at the palace of Lord Rama and Devi Sita. Interestingly, these pets are not mentioned in any other palace in Ayodhya. Can you guess what they may be?

28

Other Pets at
Prince Rama's Palace

Sage Valmiki distinguishes between the palace of Prince Rama and Emperor Dasharatha by mentioning more animals as pets. The description of the palace is mentioned when Sumantra, Dasharatha's charioteer, enters Lord Rama's palace. At that time, Lord Rama was married to Devi Sita.

In the following *shloka,* Valmiki says, 'That palace of the great souled Rama was like Indra's palace with great wealth. It was filled with various deers and peacocks (implying both numbers and types). After approaching that palace, he (Sumantra) became quite thrilled.'

Here, Valmiki uses the word *mR^igaiH,* which means deer. While, *mR^igaiH* is also used as a synonym for all four-legged grazing animals found in jungles, in this case it is specifically the deer. The following is the corresponding *shloka* from *Ayodhya Kanda, sarga* 15.

ततस्समासाद्य महाधनं महत् |
प्रहृष्टरोमा स बभूव सारथिः |
मृगैर्मयूरैश्च समाकुलोल्बणं |
गृहं वराहस्य शचीपतेरिव || २-१५-४२

tataH samaasaadya mahaadhanam mahat |
prahR^ishhTa romaa sa babhuuva saarathiH |
mR^igaiH mayuuraishcha samaakulolbaNam |
gR^iham varaarhasya shachiipataH iva II 2-15-42

Valmiki, in the next *shloka*, names another variety of
Prince Rama's pets. The exact translation of this *shloka*
from *Ayodhya Kanda* is, 'Rama's palace was as high as
the top of the Meru Mountain, shining with radiance.
The mansion was filled with birds and antelopes. It was
like Indra's mansion. Sumantra saw such a beautiful
house of Rama.'

महेंद्रसद्मप्रतिमं तु वेश्म |
रामस्य रम्यं मृगमुच्चं |
विभ्राजमानं प्रभया सुमन्त्रः || २-१५-४५

mahendrasadmapratimam tu veshma |
raamasya ramya mR^igam muchcham |
vibhraajamaanam prabhayaa sumantraH || 2-15-45

Prince Rama and Devi Sita were not only fond of birds
but also deer and antelopes.

What Is the Difference between a Deer and an
Antelope?

The differences between deer and antelopes have been
mentioned in Hindu scriptures. In various places, the
term 'great deer' or *maha mR^iga* is used for antelopes,
perhaps, because they are considered a greater species

of deer. Examples of antelopes in present-day India are *nilgai*, *chinkara* and blackbuck.

One major difference between the two is that the horns of the antelope are permanent and those of the deer are not. Deer shed their horns yearly, whereas antelope horns are permanent and consist of a perennial living bone covered with strong, thick layers of dead horn tissue. Certain types of deer, such as the musk deer have no horns. If a deer has horns, they are branched, whereas an antelope's are not. Examples of deer are red deer, *chital*, axis deer and *barasingha*.

To illustrate the differences between a tall-horned antelope and a deer, images of both are shared below. The first image, captured by Kalyan Varma and sourced from his website (www.kalyanvarma.net), is of an antelope called blackbuck. The female blackbuck has no horns.

The next image is of the Alpine Musk Deer sourced from the Smithsonian Libraries. This shy creature has no horns but instead, has small tusks. This particular species is native to the eastern Himalayas in Nepal, Bhutan and India. Another similar species, the Himalayan Musk Deer, is the state animal of Uttarakhand in India.

Many people who have not read the original Valmiki Ramayana are often left wondering why Devi Sita requests Lord Rama for a golden deer that she spots near her residence in the jungle. Some people are unable to connect the dots and, as a result, there are various distortions of the story. One such distortion that recurs is that Devi Sita requested the golden deer because she wanted to eat it. In the next chapter, we will know why exactly she wants the deer.

29

Why Does Devi Sita Request Lord Rama to Get Her the Golden Deer?

The Valmiki Ramayana is a story full of twists and turns; one such turn comes when Devi Sita spots a golden deer in the forest that she, her husband Lord Rama and brother-in-law Lakshmana are living in. She does not know that that deer is not an ordinary one, but a shape-shifting demon called Maareecha who has transformed himself into a golden deer at the behest of Ravana, the reigning monarch of demons.

When she spots the deer, she turns to Lord Rama and says, 'Oh attractive *arya putra* (son of *arya*), this deer has captivated my mind. Oh, the great armed one, fetch this animal for me, it will be our plaything in the future.' The corresponding *shloka* from the *Aranya Kanda* of Valmiki Ramayana, *sarga* 43, is shared here. The painting of the deer is done by artist Niwat.

मृगो हरति मे मनः, क्रीडार्थम् नः
भविष्यति

आर्यपुत्र अभिरामो असौ मृगो हरति मे मनः ।
आनय एनम् महाबाहो क्रीडार्थम् नः भविष्यति ॥ ३-४३-१०

aarya putra abhiraamaH asau mR^igaH harati me
manaH |
aanaya enam mahaabaahuH kriiDa artham naH
bhaviSyati | | 3-43-10

Many other *shlokas* describe Devi Sita negotiating with
Lord Rama to get her this deer to play with. She also
wishes to take it back to Ayodhya to play with in the
palace where this deer would be their prized possession,
amongst all other deer and antelopes. She further
mentions that once at the palace, this deer would bring
amazement to her brother-in-law Bharata as well as her
mothers-in-law. Devi Sita weighs all the possibilities
and asks Lord Rama that if he is not able to capture the
deer alive, he could bring back its gorgeous deerskin.
The golden deerskin could then be laid on a seat of
tender *darbha* grass-blades on which she and Lord
Rama would sit together.

According to the laws of ancient Bharat, people
who have taken a vow or are in the forest for penance
sit on a particular kind of seat. It is covered with or
made with *darbha*, the sacred grass, and if available, a

deerskin atop it. It is said that deerskin repels insects and mites that often disturb people while sitting and meditating on the floor. If deer skin is not available, the seat of *darbha* grass is covered with either wool, silk, cotton or any other animal skin. It is said that this *darbha* (seat) aids in meditation and protects the person who sits on it from all sorts of negative spiritual energies. *Darbha* grass itself is identified with Lord Vishnu and is believed to possess the power to purify anything. Because of its numerous qualities, it is an essential part of Hindu rituals.

These negotiations and discussions on how eagerly Devi Sita desires the golden deer carry on through many more *shlokas*. But in none of them does she wish to eat the deer. In fact, if read properly and in context, Devi Sita seems to be extremely fond of animals like deer and antelope, which is why even her palace in Ayodhya is filled with these animals as pets.

फलश्रुति

PHALASHRUTI

पुत्रकामश्च पुत्रान्वै धनकामो धनानि च |
लभते मनुजो लोके श्रुत्वा रामाभिषेचनम् ||
महीं विजयते राजा रिपूंश्चाप्यधितिष्ठति |

putrakAmashcha putrAnvai dhanakAmo dhanAni cha |
labhate manujo loke shrutvA rAmAbhiShechanam ||
mahIM vijayate rAjA ripUMshchApyadhitiShThati |

On hearing the narrative of his coronation in this world, a person seeking children gets children. A person looking for wealth gets riches. A king conquers the world and overcomes his enemies.

Phalashruti in Sanskrit means the fruit of listening. This implies the effect of listening or reading about a particular work, specifically about a deity or something of *dharmic* significance. Whenever we expose our minds to different things, whether we are aware or unaware, these affect our consciousness. Therefore, the images our conscious mind holds and slowly transfers to our subconscious mind will manifest in our lives. Exposing ourselves to positive things yields positive results and vice versa. Reading good books, thinking positively, listening to stories of devis and *devatas*, chanting the mantras or holy names of one's favourite deity and partaking in activities that elevate us, invariably yields good results sooner than later—just like keeping bad company will invariably rub off and land one in trouble. For this reason, most *dharmic* works have a *phalashruti* at the end.

Just like in ancient times, modern-day writers, too, secretly bless their books with certain positive affirmations to benefit their readers, which, in turn, works to their advantage. Since, I have worked on a topic of *dharmic* significance, I have chosen to follow the ancients and openly write the blessings that come with the reading of this book, rather than secretly imbibing it.

The above *phalashruti* is from the Valmiki Ramayana itself and was the closest I could find to the benefits that would match the readers of this book. The coronation of Lord Rama indicates various things: victory over enemies, opulence and kinship and the uniting of Devi Sita and Lord Rama. For this reason, the above-mentioned *phalashruti* is written in the Valmiki Ramayana. Similarly, this book, too, describes the opulence of Ayodhya, its strength over its enemies due to its fortifications and its gorgeous palaces, including that of Crown Prince Rama and his consort Crown Princess Sita when they cohabited in Ayodhya.

Therefore, those desirous of possessing wealth will be blessed with riches. Those desirous of having children will be blessed with children, since children are only born after a man and a woman come together. In the *shloka*, the Sanskrit word पुत्र (*putra*) refers to both sons and daughters, just like the word पितृ (*pitRRi*) refers to ancestors on both the mother's and father's side. Those desirous of kingship, that is, power, will be enthroned with it and those wanting victory, will be rewarded with the subjugation of enemies.

While blessings are openly stated as *phalashruti*, I would like to add a word of caution that is only valid for the person who purchases original copies of the book for their own reading or for the purposes of gifting.

Just like a property that is squatted on does not become the squatter's property and the abducted wife of another man cannot belong to the abductor, stolen knowledge never yields results.

Hindu history is replete with stories of misfortune when people engaged in such acts: for the act of abducting Devi Sita, an incarnation of the goddess of wealth herself, the mighty King Ravana lost not only his kingdom but his race of *rakshasas* was wiped off the face of this earth, and Karna, for having tricked Lord Parshurama in teaching him the knowledge of weapons, ultimately couldn't remember it when he needed it the most and as a result, died in the Mahabharata war.

A book not only contains knowledge but is also the result of years of labour of an author, the publisher and the innumerable people involved in its sales and distribution. Reading a book without paying for it via unauthorised digitised copies or buying cheap priced reproductions of books, sold by hawkers, too, will result in misfortune because one is indulging in theft of knowledge and wealth. Not only does it deprive the numerous people involved in the publishing chain of their rightly deserved wealth but it also tantamounts to theft of the author's knowledge. Therefore, such acts accrue misfortune and numerous blessings are invalidated automatically.

AFTERWORD

While writing this book and preparing for the talk I gave on the same subject, I would often discuss its content with my friends. One of the questions most people always asked me is: How do you know so much? How are you so certain that this definition is correct and the other not? How do you know these particular details?

At the beginning of this book, I have already mentioned what started me on this path. I write this afterword because I think many readers will have the same questions. The first reason that I know so many things is because I actually made an effort to travel, learn and read about a lot of other ancient cultures. This knowledge helped me understand the commonalities between ancient Hindus and the other indigenous traditions around the world, which sadly, are now in museums.

It was this interest in ancient cultures and my quest to research them that took me to Peru in 2011. I talk of gold cladding in the book, which existed in other cultures too. I had seen some examples of gold cladding myself when in Peru. Exploring Peru and learning about pre-Incan cultures helped me get a better understanding of Ayodhya. It is my opinion that most English commentators could not have imagined a stupendous district like Ayodhya to exist, a district described to have had walls of gold. And, as a result, they omitted mentioning gold-plated walls from their translations, except the Gita Press, version of the Valmiki Ramayana.

I was present at the Cusco Town Square on the New Year's Eve of 2012 when the perambulation was taking place and had joined their ritual myself. I was able to identify this as an ancient practice of perambulation around the *garbha griha* of a town.

My father, Major General Surendra Pratap Narayan Bhardwaj Rai, was the Indian Defence Advisor to various countries in North Africa and Cyprus from 1998–2002. With my parents, I had the opportunity to spend a lot of time in Egypt and explore the pyramids and temples of ancient Egyptians. I learnt a lot about the matriarchal society of ancient Egypt and the similarities between their and our temples. Even their pandits sported a *shikha* like ours. The worshipping equipment that we find in our temples nowadays were on display in the museums of Egypt. The names of the mummies were uncannily Sanskritised. I clearly remember one pharaoh who was called Shashank, a popular name for Hindus boys even today. Even Egyptians used to practice the system of gold cladding inside tombs and temples.

While one may expect a bit of an overlap, I was rather surprised at the huge number of similarities between various ancient cultures. Later on, I read many books and discussed these topics with many people who possessed a deep knowledge of ancient civilisations, including Hinduism. It was clear in my mind that either Hinduism was more widespread in the past (than we know) or that most ancient cultures practised a way of life similar to what is known as Hinduism today.

During my decade-long stay in foreign countries, I made friends with people of various nationalities and made attempts to learn about them. In one of those stays, I became good friends with a tall Dutch gentleman called Sip whose wife, like him, was a tall and sweet lady by the name of Sita. I was intrigued about her name and asked if she knew what the name meant. She said, 'No, I do not know what it means, but it is a traditional Dutch name too.' She further added, 'Many Indians have asked me the same and are quite surprised at my name.' I could understand the surprise, as Sita is the name of a revered ancient Hindu queen and incarnation of Goddess Lakshmi, the goddess of wealth. Their friendship exposed me to the possibility of really tall people existing on planet Earth. I had read in books and heard in stories of *itihasa* that Hindus in the previous yugas were really tall, specially the *yoddhas* (fighters) and *devatas*, who averaged almost 7 feet or more, like Ashwatthama (grandson of Rishi Bhardwaj) and Lord Parashuram. Both these Brahmin warriors were known for their extreme physical strength. Before I met Sip and Sita, I used to take these stories with a pinch of salt and afterwards I realised that maybe it was me who has yet to explore all that exists in the world before I assume the truths written in scriptures as exaggerated.

The second reason is my own thirst for knowledge about ancient cultures. As a child, I was not interested in Nancy Drew as much as I was in decoding the mysteries of the ancient world. I would rather pick a book like the *Chariot of the Gods* by Erich Von Daniken over other teenybopper books. I had read this book by the time I was in grade five even though I did not understand the English properly or was able to locate the countries mentioned in the book on the map. That is why I have written this book in very simple English and have included many images, so that children can easily understand what is being conveyed. If they do not understand Sanskrit or English words or their meanings, they can always understand with the help of images. This will not only enhance their knowledge but also their vocabulary.

The third reason is my own lineage. My last name is Rai, which is spelt as *raya* or *raja* in Sanskrit and means 'king'. The word also means various types of riches. This surname was originally a prefix meant to signify a king. Brahmins who have this surname hail from a martial clan called Bhumi Kara Brahmins, popularly known as Bhumihar Brahmins. This clan of Brahmins draws its lineage from the sixth avatar of Vishnu, Lord Parshurama, who, after killing Emperor Sahastra Arjuna and his 1,000 *samanta rajas* (privicial kings), had appointed his Brahmin students as the rulers of the land of the Vindhya ranges.

Growing up, my maternal and paternal grandmothers, both daughters of wealthy zamindars or *samant rajas*, had a huge role to play in increasing my knowledge about ancient Hindus. I used to listen to their stories and was rather fascinated by the lives they led. The kind of real-life stories I heard from my *naani* and *daadi* are the stories that are now relegated only to history books and old photographs of ancient Bharat.

An example is of my *naani*'s father. Growing up in Kundesar, a district of Gazipur (Uttar Pradesh), she herself used to travel in palanquins, but her father often travelled on the back of an elephant. Once his elephant would not allow him to ride, so he bought a camel and rode it. When this happened, the elephant realised that he was not the most important animal in the house and that he could be replaced. After this incident, my great grandfather's elephant always behaved well and threw no tantrums.

When I first heard this story, I was utterly amused to learn that even animals suffered from jealousy. To me, it was just a funny story. At this point, I did not know much about the wealth or status of an individual to be able to possess numerous animals. It was much later that I learnt what it meant to own elephants and camels back in the day. For me, these were just stories that I heard growing up. Therefore, when Valmiki speaks about the elephants owned by the kings and about the rich citizens of Ayodhya owning, at least, a cow and a horse, I can truly understand his comparisons.

The ownership of elephants by kings and their usage as war animals in Hindu armies of the past are comparable to modern folks owning expensive luxury cars. So much so, that if someone is rich and does not have a nice ride, then people suspect whether he is truly wealthy. These things are so deeply rooted in our consciousness that even children are aware of it. Another funny anecdote that occurred around this accepted fact happened in my family where my father, a young boy of five years, pointed out this truth to his father about his father's friend. My grandfather,

Lt Colonel Shyam Sundar Rai, was posted in Faridkot, Punjab, as a Captain in National Cadet Corps (NCC) where the Maharaja of Faridkot, Harinder Singh Brar, also an army officer, was his friend. He was the Honorary Colonel of the regiment of the Sikh Light Infantry, senior to my grandfather in rank and rather fond of him.

Since my grandfather, too, was commissioned in the same regiment and there was a good comraderie between both the men, my grandparents would often pay the maharaja a visit on the weekends at his palace, taking my father and his siblings along. Faridkot was one of the richest princely states of India. In the palace, the maharaja had numerous preserved animals like the tiger on display. He also had many pet dogs.

During one such meeting, my father told my grandfather, 'What sort of a king is he who has no elephants but only stuffed animals in his palace?' Since my grandparents had an elephant back home, my father assumed he must be a fake king or an imposter. The stuffed animals he referred to were taxidermied. When my grandfather conveyed my father's thoughts to the maharaja, both of them couldn't stop laughing.

Later, this became a joke between the two men and everytime they would catch up, they would repeat it amongst themselves. The maharaja remembered this joke for a very long time. Many years after this incident, he visited Meerut in 1966–1967 for the Bienniel Conference of the Sikh Light Infantry Regiment. At that time, my grandfather was posted as the Deputy Commandant of Sikh Light Regiment Centre in the city. When they caught up, the maharaja repeated the same joke to my grandfather and asked to especially meet his son who had questioned his rulership. My grandfather had five sons and by then, my father was in the 11th standard. On meeting my father, they all had a hearty laugh.

Another anecdote I clearly remember, which made sense to me only after I read the Valmiki Ramayana, was the 'chicken story'. During my holidays, I would often stay with my maternal grandparents. My *naani* would routinely ask me what I'd like to eat. It so happened that within a short span of time, I requested to eat chicken twice. The second time I did, my grandmother snapped at me and said, 'You keep discussing dharma and karma with me all day long and then you want to eat chicken?'

I was rather puzzled at her reaction and innocently replied, 'Yes, so?'

'Don't you know that Hindus do not eat birds?'

'Then what should I eat?' I asked her quizzically.

'Eat what Kashmiri Pandits eat if you wish to eat meat. Eat goats.' My vegetarian *naani* replied in a huff as she walked off to do her chores.

This interaction had left me completely bewildered. It was not until I read the Valmiki Ramayana that I understood what my *naani* was trying to convey. Since Hindus in the past (especially royalty) used to keep birds as pets, eating them was forbidden. According to her, a better option was to eat four-legged animals like goats. It is only now that the concept of having cats and dogs as pets is in vogue; in earlier times, birds and cows were favoured as pets by Hindus. Therefore, my choice of food was considered sacrilegious.

Considering I was brought up in a rather liberal atmosphere, it was not possible for me to learn these things from my surroundings, where eating everything except for beef or buff was kosher. Only when I learnt about the birds reared by the royals at the palaces did I understand what my grandmother was trying to convey. There must have been some ancient wisdom in Hindus choosing not to eat birds which we have lost to time.

Similarly, I learnt much from the wisdom of my grandmother's stories about dharma and our family lineage. My great great grandfather (*naani*'s paternal grandfather) was the famous wrestler Zamindar Hari Narayan Singh from Kundesar, who was world-renowned back in the day for killing a man-eating tiger with his bare hands. It was because of his father's hobby and passion for wrestling that led Hari Narayan to be trained as a wrestler from an early age. The father-son duo indulged in this art form for their love of it. I grew up listening to stories of my great great grandfather's strength and prowess. He is probably the strongest man to have lived in modern India. Various people have written articles and books on him, of which the most famous one is *The Last Wrestlers* by martial artiste Marcus Trower. Zamindar Hari Narayan Singh was a polyglot and was fluent in Sanskrit apart from, at least, the three other languages: Hindi, Bhojpuri, Farsi. In the articles and stories about him, many people have written that he had memorised the Bhagavad Gita, but few know that he used to recite it every day from memory. It was a part of his daily routine. Not only was he immensely strong, but also very *dharmic* and spiritual. Before he died, he had informed his family that his time had come and he then moved to Kashi (modern-day Varanasi) so he could die there. Many devout Hindus desire to die in Kashi and other specific places of pilgrimage so that their soul breaks from the chain of life and death, and they are never reborn. Once they reach there, they partake in *dharmic* practices and spend their time in devotion to the devis and *devatas*.

In the past, a thorough knowledge of *dharmic* scriptures and Sanskrit was a must for Hindu royals. Emperor Dasharatha, too, was well versed in the Vedas, as stated by Sage Valmiki. Great physical strength and the ability to fight and hunt tough animals in the wild used to be a prized attribute of men. In the Ramayana, too, various *shlokas* mention that Lord Rama's chariot had shiny tiger skins. The skin of any animal remains shiny when it has been hunted recently. This is why these *shlokas* have been mentioned in the Ramayana.

Hunting used to be a common activity for all royals. They were not only hunted for their skin but also for their various uses. Once I had fallen sick and was unable to recover properly. So my innocent *daadi* (paternal grandmother) suggested to me, 'Child, see if you can hunt two tigers from somewhere. If not, ask your friends to obtain it for you. Many years ago when I was a young girl, both my maternal aunt and I fell very sick. So the *vaidya* recommended obtaining two tigers to treat us. Therefore, my father promptly hunted two tigers. After using the directives of the *vaidya* for the treatment, I till date have not fallen sick with that ailment.'

At that I laughed and reminded her that it was illegal to kill a tiger now. She replied, 'Oh, my father used to go on hunting expeditions. Often with the British too. It was allowed in those days.'

I replied laughingly, 'Yes, but it is illegal now. You sure do not want me to go to jail, do you?'

I, of course, do not condone the killing of animals for any sort of medicinal purpose and this example is only presented to show the ease and acceptane of hunting as a dangerous sport or hobby practised by the royals of the past. Apart from guns, they used to get trained in unarmed combat, too, which enabled them to fight both enemies and animals. A specific grappling technique of hand-to-hand combat and wrestling empowered my great great grandfather Zamindar Hari Narayan Singh to kill a man-eating tiger with his bare hands.

I mention these stories because my generation is the bridge between the past and the future. Those who come after us may consider all this as fiction because of lack of documentation and mention in books. The breaks between tradition and gaps between generations, which go undocumented, lead to fallacies like Hindu *itihasa* being called mythological.

I hope that the mystery of how I know so much is resolved to some extent. I also hope that the future generation is as honest to the scriptures as I have been to them and my lineage. Bringing dishonesty to Hindu scriptures is equivalent to changing the meanings of words or explaining different meanings in order to sail with the popular opinion of the day. One should clearly state scriptures as they are with their correct meanings and possible explanations to events and phenomena that are no longer in common practice.

Conceptualising and creating this book was like maneuvering through unexplored territory and through it all, I enjoyed the support of my parents and the benevolence of two Sanskrit guides, Shri B.P. Pandey and Dr Sanjay Jha, both of whom helped me sail through the vast ocean of scriptural knowledge encoded in *shlokas*.

I hope that you enjoyed the book. I have a lot of material for other books and I am in the process of putting them to paper. I would love to share these books (when completed) with you. For a better understanding of Ayodhya, I recommend that you watch my talk on the same subject too. Forgive me for any error that I may have failed to correct. This book was completed in the lockdown following the Covid-19 pandemic, when I did not have proper access to libraries for research work.

The pandemic has been a painful time for everyone, including me. It has been a time of losses at many levels and it caused considerable delays in getting this book out. During this time, I lost an uncle suddenly to dengue. Ten days after his death, I lost my beloved cat Puma to bilateral renal failure on the night of Dussehra. Very few people understand the attachment to pets and their presence in one's life in the form of a child. Puma was a rescued cat who had been a faithful, loving and affectionate childlike pet for 10 years. He followed me about the house like a lamb. Whenever I worked through the night on the manuscript, he used to sit right behind my laptop like a sphinx guarding the great pyramids. As time went by and his health deteriorated, he was no longer able to sit and so he would curl up to sleep behind the laptop. Either way, he never left me alone for a moment through good or bad times.

Many friends and well-wishers were waiting eagerly for this book and did not know the real reason behind its delay. Therefore, I have chosen to inform about it in the book itself. Please accept my apologies for the delay. Some friends were disturbed that Puma died on Dussehra. Even though his loss bothers me tremendously, there could be no better day for him to leave. All that is born has to die one day because death is the only constant in this world. As a devotee of Lord Rama and Devi Sita, if the lord wished to indicate that my beloved pet was safe with him, which better day would He have chosen to indicate that Puma was indeed under his protection? In my opinion, it could only have been days that are of significance to Lord Rama, namely Dussehra or Diwali. These are small but immensely comforting signals for a devotee in times of grief. This incident further strengthened my belief that Lord Rama and Devi Sita always shower their blessings and grace upon devotees.

Jai Siya Rama

Amazing Ayodhya captures the narration of the grandeur of Ayodhya as described in the Valmiki Ramayan. For my research, I have referred to the below-mentioned sources. I would like to render a heartfelt thanks to all all the sources online and otherwise, that have enabled people like me to study the scriptures. These have been excellent sources of research and understanding the Valmiki Ramayana.

For the Valmiki Ramayana

There are many sources for research work on Ayodhya, and one of the best is the Gita Press Ramayana, Gorakhpur. This particular Valmiki Ramayana was printed by Hanuman Prasad Poddar in 1960. The *tikakaar* of this translation is Pandit Ram Narayan Dutt Shastri Pandey 'Ram'. The *tika* is in Hindi and in places this translation uses *tikas* from other learned pandits as well. *Tikakaar,* for a work in Sanskrit, like the Ramayana, means a person who gives a commentary, translates and explains with meaning. A newer version of the Valmiki Ramayana from the Gita Press was also referred to. The preface of this version was given by Janaki Nath Sharma.

Many versions of Valmiki Ramayana are also available online. One of the online versions in English is from the Indian Institute of Technology, Kanpur. On their website they have stated: There are several commentaries on Valmiki Ramayana. However, six of the important commentaries have been selected for translation. The selected commentaries and the names of the translators are as follows. The Southern recession of Ramayana has been adopted by the project.

+ *Govinda Raja Pranita Ramayana Bhusana*
+ *Shree Madhava Yogi Pranita Amritakataka*
+ *Shiva Sahaya Pranita Ramayana Siromani*
+ *Rama Pranita Ramayana Tilaka*
+ *Maheswara Thirtha*
+ *Dhrmakuta*

Another version of Valmiki Ramayana in English is available at www.valmikiramayan.net. This version is translated and presented by Sri Desiraju Hanumanta Rao and Sri K.M.K. Murthy. These different sources are used so the reader gets a proper picture of Ayodhya, as described by *Ādi Kavi* Valmiki. It is pertinent to remember that there are various versions of the Valmiki Ramayana, namely the Northwest, East and South versions. These versions have nominal variations in the usage of certain words. The Sanskrit *shlokas* used in the book have been sourced from sanskritdocuments.org.

For the Images

Most of the images sourced by me are copyright-free from Wikipedia or various other online image banks. I have mentioned the name of the photographer or illustrator (or source) with the text of the book. I am forever grateful to creative people who share their talent and creations with others.

The images used are purely for illustrative purposes because it is near impossible to convey through words the graphic details about an era long gone and only transferred via the oral culture of the Hindus.

BIBLIOGRAPHY

Articles

'Antelope vs. Deer', Diffen.com, 18 February 2021, https://www.diffen.com/difference/Antelope_vs_Deer

'Bhagavad Gita: The Song of God', commentary by Swami Mukudananda, https://www.holy-bhagavad-gita.org

G. Siromoney, M. Bagavandas and S. Govindaraju, 'An iconometric study of Pallava sculptures', *Kalakshetra Quarterly*, Vol. 3 No. 2, 1980, pp. 7–15, https://www.cmi.ac.in/gift/Iconometry/icon_pallavasculpture.htm

'Hippos: Life force of African rivers', Voice of Africa, 2 May 2015, https://learningenglish.voanews.com/a/hippos-life-force-of-african-rivers/2733549.html

http://newdelhi.thaiembassy.org/en/2018/07/kings-india-royal-thai-family-context-siam-bharat-relations/

http://www.detailsofindia.com/symbols-of-india/jharkhand-sal-tree/

https://www.backyardbuddies.org.au/backyard-buddies/bush-stone-curlew

https://www.diffen.com/difference/Antelope_vs_Deer

https://www.visitjanakpur.com/

ITRANS Transliteration Map, https://sanskritdocuments.org/dict/itrans.html

Pacha, A. 'History of India's last known hippo', *The Hindu*, 19 January 2019, https://www.thehindu.com/sci-tech/science/history-of-indias-last-known-hippo/article26037560.ece

Shamasastry R., 'Kautilya Arthashastra', *Wisdom Library*, https://www.wisdomlib.org/hinduism/book/kautilya-arthashastra/d/doc366064.html#note-e-128493

Subramanian T.S., 'The Rise and Fall of a Harappan City', *Frontline*, 18 June 2020, https://frontlinhttp://ignca.gov.in/Asi_data/22949.pdfe.thehindu.com/static/html/fl2712/stories/20100618271206200.htm

Wee, R.Y., 'What is the Tallest Country in the World?' World Atlas, 7 August 2018, https://www.worldatlas.com/articles/countries-with-the-tallest-average-heights.html

पौराणिक चतुरंगिणी एवं अक्षौहिणी सेना क्या थी ? / मानसश्री डॉ.नरेन्द्रकुमार मेहता, https://www.rachanakar.org/2017/03/blog-post_487.html

Books

Acharya, Prasanna Kumar, *Architecture of Manasara Shilpshastra*, (Oxford University Press: London, 1933)

Acharya, Prassana Kumar, *Dictionary of Hindu Architecture*, (New Delhi: Low Price Publications, 1934).

Dave, K.N., *Birds in Sanskrit Literature*, (New Delhi: Motilal Banarasidass Publishers Pvt. Ltd, 2005).

Raz, Ram, *Essay on the Architecture of the Hindus*, (London: The Royal Asiatic Society of Great Britain and Ireland, 1834)

Shamasastry R., *Kautilya Arthashastra*, (Mysore: Mysore Printing and Publishing House, 1956).

Shukla, R.K., *The Geography of the Ramayana*, (New Delhi: Koshal Book Depot, 2003).

Sinha, Sushil Kumar, *The Bhumihars, Caste of Eastern India*, (New Delhi: Raj Publications, 2019).

Neena Rai was born in Pune, India, and now lives in New Delhi. She is an alumna of the prestigious Indian Institute of Mass Communication, New Delhi. After completing her post-graduation, she left India to pursue work in the Middle East. Over a decade later, she decided to move back to India to contribute to the country and its people.

Neena is passionate about writing and understanding the wisdom contained in the Hindu scriptures. She has been studying Sanskrit for many years to understand *dharmic* texts better. She is a devotee of Lord Rama and Devi Sita. She likes poetry, and reading both fiction and nonfiction. She is also an accomplished abstract artist. In the past, apart from working in the media, she has also worked as a fashion model and an international flight attendant. She currently runs a business in New Delhi.

In her free time, she loves doing yoga, gardening and watching movies.